Contents

The numbered items are discussion briefs

Introduction   1
  1 Courtesies and professionalism in school   5

Part One   7

SECTION ONE: SCHOOL NOTEBOOK

Purpose and professionalism in keeping a school notebook   9
  2 School notebook – preliminary guidelines   9
Use of the school notebook during stage one: participant observation   10
  3 First day observations – extract from a notebook   11
  4 Participant observation – extract from a notebook   12
  5 Drawing classroom plans   13
Use of the school notebook during stage two: 'one group' teaching   14
  6 Infants, stage two teaching – extract from a notebook I   15
  7 Infants, stage two teaching – extract from a notebook II   16
  8 Juniors, stage two teaching – extract from a notebook I   18
  9 Juniors, stage two teaching – extract from a notebook II   18
 10 Forecasts and evaluations of teaching – objectives, strategies
     and resources   20
Group planning exercises for stage two   22
 11 Planning work for a group of infants   22
 12 Planning a lesson for a junior class   23
*Use of the school notebook during stage three: 'more than one
group' teaching*   23
 13 Stage three teaching – extract from a notebook   24
Children's educational needs and teachers' objectives   26
 14 Children's educational needs in general   27
 15 Individual children's educational needs   28

Ascertaining children's needs   29
16   Classroom observation of children in small groups   29
Patterns of classroom and team teaching organization   30
17   Four patterns of classroom organization   31
18   Five patterns of team teaching organization   32
19   Classroom observation of a teacher   33
School notebooks for stage four: 'most of the children for most of the time'   35
20   School notebooks, stage four teaching, I   35
21   Overall forecast, stage four teaching – extract from a notebook   38
22   Records of individual children   39
23   Daily records – three way tick book   41
24   Curriculum forecast for six weeks, stage four teaching – extract from a notebook   42
25   Daily forecast, stage four teaching – extract from a notebook   50
26   School notebooks, stage four teaching, II   52

SECTION TWO: CLASSROOM CONTROL   55
27   Children's expectations of their teacher   56
28   Personal power of a teacher   57
29   Organization   58
30   Noise   59
31   Instructions   60
32   Punishment   61
33   What to try with a disruptive child   63
34   What to try if a riot breaks out   65
35   Classroom control simulation 1 – 'Story time'   67
36   Classroom control simulation 2 – 'Matchsticks'   68
37   Classroom control simulation 3 – 'Getting cross'   69

SECTION THREE: CLASSROOM SKILLS   71
38   Printing and handwriting   71
39   Work cards   73
40   Classroom display   75
41   Classroom A/V aids   76
42   Telling and reading stories   77
43   Classroom discussions   79
44   Marking and motivating in the classroom   82
45   Curriculum organization – objectives, strategies and problems   83

SECTION FOUR: ANALYSING AND EVALUATING ONE'S OWN TEACHING   89

46   Evaluating a single teaching event   90
47   Evaluating continuous teaching   90

Part Two   93

Case study 1   Class teaching by 'the traditional day'   98
Case study 2   Class teaching by 'the integrated day'   111
Case study 3   Class teaching by 'groupwork'   129
Case study 4   Team teaching by 'groupwork'   144
Case study 5   Team teaching by 'individual work'   150

End piece   159

Index   163

Acknowledgments

The ideas contained in this book have slowly come together during the last five years and in particular have developed through my experience as a school tutor working on the CNAA Generalist B.Ed. at York House, Trent Polytechnic.

Many students, teachers and fellow tutors have contributed in different ways to the making of this book, amongst whom I would like to mention: George Andrew, David Burns, Margery Cree, Sam Ellis, Sue Everatt, Jane Green, Barbara Hardy, Nina Hatch, John Lesquereux, Sheila Mellors, John Parsons, Heather Sparrow, Mary Spencer, Norma Taylor, Pat Walsh, Connie Winsor and Lottie Woolridge.

My especial thanks are due to Pamela Quaintmere, who opened my eyes to many facets of teaching and in particular suggested what I believe to be the most important idea in the book – the three kinds of tick of brief 23; and to Paul Leigh, who allowed me to adapt some of his teaching documents, and who gave me the encouragement of friendly criticism.

I am conscious that the text will be found to contain naïvetés; for these the reader must hold me responsible. I shall welcome correspondence aimed at improving the text.

Michael Bassey
Trent Polytechnic Nottingham

Introduction

Teaching in a contemporary primary school is extraordinarily demanding; it is also one of the most satisfying occupations. It requires energy, sensitivity, empathy, intelligence, creativeness, adaptability, persistence, and patience. It requires detailed curriculum knowledge of language, mathematics, art and craft, music, physical education, etc. and a broad cultural base of general knowledge. It also requires a high order of organizational skills if the resources for learning are to be used to the best advantage of each individual child; it is with these classroom organizational skills that this book is concerned.

The purpose of the book is to stimulate and guide the thinking of student-teachers on the skills of classroom organization; it can serve the same purposes for teachers in their early years of teaching.

The book is concerned with the training of primary school teachers. Although some of the material may be appropriate for students intending to teach in secondary schools, in general the differences between primary and secondary education are such that attempts to encompass both in suggestions for student-teachers, fail to grapple effectively with the day-to-day business of teaching. Indeed, the differences between the needs of infant and junior teachers are not inconsiderable and special emphases are required. For the same reason no reference to nursery teaching is made.

Probably some readers will frown at the word 'training'. I use it to refer to that part of a student-teacher's education in which teaching skills are learned through discussion and practice. The book is intended as a source book for students, tutors, for teachers in relation to students working with them and, to some extent, for teachers themselves in terms of their own professional development. The text is variously addressed to these groups. I believe that it is unhelpful in higher education to try to write one book for tutor and another for student. Teacher training needs to be a partnership between students, tutors and school teachers with common objectives and, as such, it is obviously helpful for the different partners to know what the others are trying to do.

It is not expected that students will read the book straight through, but rather that it will be used as a collection of resources which can form starting points for discussion. Part of the art of the tutor is to stimulate discussion at the appropriate time. For example, a discussion on classroom discipline may fail to arouse interest if it is held before students have worked in school, or, even worse, may lead to antipathy and rejection of the topic. On the other hand, it can be a valuable help if it is introduced just at the time when some students are first meeting classroom difficulties.

The book is divided into two parts. Part One contains a series of forty-seven briefs for student discussion, stitched together with comments about the briefs which are designed for tutors. The briefs have been written with few words, so that they can be read quickly. They can be studied by someone working alone, but in general, more will be gained if they form the focus for the discussion of a group. Some points are contentious and it is to be expected that tutors and students, as well as teachers and heads, will disagree with some of the points expressed. If this stimulates further thought about the practice of teaching it is worthwhile. Most of the briefs require no more than a preliminary reading before discussion, but in a few cases activities are suggested prior to discussion.

Part Two contains five case studies of the day-by-day work of some primary school teachers, written to draw attention to organizational practice. Anyone who rejects the truth of the opening sentence of this Introduction, that teaching is 'extraordinarily demanding', should be encouraged to read these case studies. Indeed, it may be profitable for many readers to examine these case studies early on, for they provide the answer to the question which many students ask 'What is the purpose of keeping a school notebook?' In order to achieve the levels of competence described in these case studies, considerable self-training is needed; this can be by steady progression through the stages described in Part One.

Some people believe that in teacher training students should be pushed in at the deep end and start teaching with a large class and a full timetable. They believe that most students will survive and through the struggle will learn what there is to learn about teaching. This book is not for deep-end plungers. I believe that students should start in the shallows and should be led steadily into the depths of teaching; to push students into deep water too early can harm them as teachers. The proper role of tutors in teacher training is the structuring of learning experiences which assist the development from acolyte to professional. Unfortunately in the past, too much tutor attention has been directed towards assessment of the student's performance and too little on helping her to perform well.

It is helpful to identify stages in the training pattern; the scheme of this book contains six stages and can be applied to the training pattern of both infant and junior teachers.

2

Stage one

Participant observation: assisting the teacher and working under his direction with activities which he has planned.

Examples of a teacher's directions to a student:

'These children are writing about witches. Talk to them individually about their writing and write words in their word books when they ask you.' (infants)

'Help this group make a collage of a swan. The materials are here and the children have already drawn an outline.' (infants)

'Everybody is working at mathematics from their Beta books. Go and help people who put their hands up.' (juniors)

'Read the next chapter of *The Wind in the Willows* to the class.' (juniors)

Stage two

'One group' teaching: planning for and working with either one group of about six children for most of a day, or with the whole class for about an hour a day where all the children are working on the same subject.

Examples of a teacher's directions to a student:

'Next Tuesday after registration and assembly I want you to work with the red group (six children) for most of the day. Plan some number work followed by writing and then by creative work. I suggest you do measuring with centimetres for the number work. Find a simple theme for writing and creative work – you can probably link them together. The group can join the rest of the class at 3 p.m. when I read a story.' (infants)

'Next Tuesday from 9.30 to playtime I want you to give a class lesson on "Time". Talk to them for a bit and then get them to write in their books. I suggest you concentrate mainly on the units of time.' (juniors)

Stage three

'More than one group' teaching: planning for and working with either about twelve children split into two or three groups for most of the day, or the whole class for an hour or more when the children are divided into several groups and engaging in different activities.

Examples of a teacher's directions to a student:

'Next Tuesday after registration and assembly I want you to work with the red group and the yellow group all day up to 3 p.m. Plan some number work, creative work and writing. I suggest you do measuring of water in pints and thirds-of-a-pint,

3

and for creative work use the clay. There is room for six children at the sinks and six on the clay table at one time.' (infants)

'Next Tuesday from 9.30 to playtime I want you to organize the class to work on "Faces". Talk with them for a few minutes and then set up several groups which work on different activities to do with the topic.' (juniors)

Stage four

'*Most of the children most of the time*': planning for and working with the children at a level up to ninety per cent of a full-time teacher's responsibility. This is the stage of the final teaching practice in an initial training course. It is not the end of a teacher's training; there is no end.

Stage five

'*Full-time teaching – just surviving*': this is the period when there is an enormous gain in experience and self-confidence. The gaps in competence at teaching basic skills are filled and routine patterns of work are established.

Stage six

'*Full-time teaching – analysing, evaluating, planning*': after the settling down period of Stage five comes the time when the teacher can focus his intelligence on the interactions between himself and his class, individually and collectively. Now he has the confidence to analyse his curriculum in relation to the educational needs of the children as individuals, to identify his objectives and to try to justify them, to evaluate his classroom resources and his teaching strategies, and to replan his work accordingly. This stage should be as long as the teacher's professional career.

Obviously, students move through these stages at different rates and in some schools it is less easy than in others to structure each stage in turn. The merit of identifying the early stages is that they provide a basis for planning a student's work in school which can be quite clear to student, teacher, headteacher and tutor. It is particularly helpful if the teacher gives clear directions to the student on what he expects her to do, along the lines suggested in the examples.

Part One provides ideas and suggestions which are relevant to Stages one to four and which provide a basis for Stage five. The case studies of Part Two give insights into five different ways of working which may be of greatest significance at Stages four and five. No specific reference to Stage six is made, but the teacher who has been trained in the kind of thinking of Part One is well equipped for the autonomous intellectual activity of this final and continuous stage of learning about teaching.

The first of the forty-seven discussion briefs follows. It is about courtesies and professionalism in school. Discussion of staff room coffee cups and whether women students can wear trousers may be trivial in relation to most schools, but in some places a mistake in these respects may mar the start of a teaching practice. Certainly punctuality and the appropriate use of names matters in all schools. This brief also serves to introduce the style of Part One.

---

1   Courtesies and professionalism in school

When you first visit a school your purpose is to observe the school. But remember that the school is also observing you! These points are worthy of discussion in a group:

(a)   The status of students in school in terms of relationships with head, teachers, tutor, children. Are adults called only by their surnames? If first names are used, when, where, who and by whom?

(b)   The importance of punctuality; after school leaving time; procedure if unable to attend.

(c)   Dress: try to conform to the norms of the school staff.

(d)   Staffroom behaviour: be sensitive to such matters as ownership of coffee mugs, paying for coffee, chairs, coat-pegs, car parking, loos.

(e)   Classroom behaviour: act in cooperation with the teacher; stop talking yourself if the teacher suddenly starts to address the whole class; beware of giving instructions to children that could lead to accidents.

(f)   Legal points: students are not permitted to punish children physically, nor to take sole responsibility for physical education involving apparatus, nor to take children outside the school grounds without the head's permission.

(g)   Emergency procedures for accidents, fires, etc.

(h)   Use of materials: don't exhaust the school's supply of paper, paint, etc!

Teaching is a demanding activity in which day-by-day a large number of decisions and judgments are made by the individual teacher; inevitably the sensitive teacher will feel that sometimes he has taken the wrong action and it doesn't help if he feels that the student observing is being critical. As a student, seek to establish a good personal relationship with any teacher with whom you work. Remember that although questions are one of the most valuable tools for your learning, people will reply only as far as they can trust you with the answers.

Before going into a school have ready some simple activities which you could use with a class of children for a short time at a moment's notice. The programme of most primary schools from time to time becomes spontaneous and you should be ready for the head saying, 'We are having a spot of bother. Could you take Mrs Brown's class for a short while? I am sure you can find something to do with them.'

Part One

Discussion briefs on classroom organization

SECTION ONE   SCHOOL NOTEBOOK

PURPOSE AND PROFESSIONALISM IN KEEPING A SCHOOL NOTEBOOK

A student's school notebook is a tool for learning how to teach. Regular writing helps her to structure her thinking in both observing children and other teachers and in planning and evaluating her own work.

The sequence of briefs in this section gives ideas and suggestions for the use of a school notebook from stage one (participant observation) to stage four ('most of the children most of the time'). The purpose and content changes considerably through this sequence, but at no stage should a student be expected to spend more than one hour a day thinking, and writing in her book, at the end of a full day in school.

I recommend a very firm guideline on the question of what form of observational comment is appropriate. Student written observations in a school notebook should be factual and should not stray into the dangerous territory of critical opinion.

It is an important aspect of the personal and professional relationship between student and school that any notes made by the student about her experience of school should be open for inspection and comment by those who are in partnership with her in her training – teacher, headteacher and tutor. Few activities can destroy personal relationships more than the making of secret notes. On the other hand, by positively presenting the notes to the teacher and asking for the correction of errors, a mutual trust and understanding can develop, and this, of course, is important for later times when the teacher is providing opportunities for the student to teach in his classroom.

2 School notebook – preliminary guidelines

You will need a school notebook or file for recording your observations of the school and, later, for planning and evaluating your own teaching and for keeping simple records of children's work. Either use a hardback notebook (which is more convenient for carrying about) or a loose-leaf file (which is more flexible). Put your name clearly on the outside. This identifies it and helps dissuade children from reading it if you have left it lying around. Before you make any entries in your book, be clear that your tutor, any class-teacher with whom you are working, and the headteacher, may want to read your notes from time to time. When you are describing the school or the work of a teacher, keep your notes factual and do not express negative or critical opinions.

Try to be systematic in your entries. This helps you when you refer back to earlier notes and also helps your tutor and teacher when they read your notebook. Some suggestions follow.

> Draw a margin to each page; this gives space for tutor or teacher, or yourself later on, to insert brief comments. Number the pages for ease of cross-reference.
> Put the date and day of the week at the top of each entry so that it can be identified later. Separate each day's entry with a line right across the page.
> Write in any style that comes easily, i.e. short notes or continuous prose, present or past tense, personal or impersonal.
> It may be helpful to refer to your teacher by using his initial, e.g. 'Mr R'. Record the names of individual children when you can, rather than statements like 'a group of children'.

After a day in school most students could write for several hours, but clearly too much writing is counter-productive. An appropriate time is about an hour for thinking and writing in your school notebook.

The purpose and content of your writing in a school notebook will change during your training. You will probably start with observations in a diary form, then begin to plan and evaluate limited amounts of teaching, and eventually plan and evaluate day-by-day teaching. Systematic habits established early on are likely to be a source of strength when you are in the maelstrom of full-time teaching.

USE OF THE SCHOOL NOTEBOOK DURING STAGE ONE: PARTICIPANT OBSERVATION

Tutor opinion differs on the extent to which it is worth structuring the initial observation of school life. Some tutors give a list of questions for students to answer, others use a discussion period to draw up a list from the suggestions of students, while others may leave students to organize their observations in their own way. Certainly for many students the first visit to a school as a student-teacher is so emotionally charged an experience that it tends to make the answering of factual questions an irrelevant activity.

One approach to deciding what to write in a notebook is to reflect on somebody else's notes. This technique is used in a number of the briefs of this section. Brief 3 contains an extract from a student's notebook and describes the experience of the first day in school as a student-teacher. Brief

4 is the notes made on a later day, but still during the stage of participant observation. These extracts are partly invented and partly about real situations.

3   First day observations – extract from a notebook

Tuesday 7 October Observation

9.30   Arrived at school and welcomed by Mr A, the headteacher. He talked to us for an hour about the school and then showed us round. We were then placed in classes: I am with Mr B who has a class of second year juniors.

10.45   We were introduced to the rest of the staff at break.

11.00   I watched Mr B give a lesson about African animals and then helped the children with their writing.

12.00   School dinner time.

1.30   Mr B had a PE lesson in the hall and then set the class to do individual work while he talked to me about his organization and curriculum.

2.45   Afternoon break

3.00   Mr B asked me to hear some readers.

3.30   Mr B read to the class from *Watership Down* by Richard Adams.

Notes about the school

The school was built in 1878 of red brick and has church-like ceilings and small windows; it is brightly painted. A new part with four classrooms was added in 1972.

It is a Church of England controlled school. There are six managers, two from the Church and four from the Education Authority; one of the Church members has to be chairman. The rector takes school assembly once a week.

About half of the children come from the immediate area of the school and their fathers are miners or work in local light-engineering factories. About a quarter come from a nearby private estate which was built a few years ago. Their fathers are mainly professional and clerical workers. The other children come from distant areas because their parents want them to attend a Church school. Overall Mr A estimates that a third of the mothers work – in factories, offices, etc.

There are 264 children in the school, aged from five to eleven. There are four infant classes and six juniors. Numbers will increase during the year.

Mr A is particularly concerned about mathematics and reading. For both of these there is a curriculum scheme which operates throughout the school.

Notes about the class

There are twenty-nine children in Mr B's class, aged eight to nine. They are not streamed; the reading ages vary from five to thirteen. Their names, reading ages, and the group to which they belong, are listed on the next page. The timetable is on page 5 of this notebook. (These details have been omitted – MB.) Each morning three of the groups do English and three do mathematics, changing on alternate days. Mathematics is based on the Beta books and the children mark a wall chart as they finish each section. Mr B has two twenty-minute class lessons each day – on mathematics, PE, topic, etc. At present the topic lessons are about animals and the children are compiling their own books about this.

Points for next week

1   Draw a plan of the classroom showing where the children sit.
2   Ask for a copy of the school's mathematics scheme.
3   What style of handwriting is expected?
4   What do the children keep in their lockers?

---

4   Participant observation – extract from a notebook

Tuesday afternoon 21 October Participant observation

1.30   Mr B said: 'Supervise that group of six who are making leaf prints.'
The children were Ann, Christopher, Melvyn, Michaela, Stephen and Tony. The resources for the group were: leaves which they had collected at dinner time, thick poster paint, white paper, paint brushes, pieces of hardboard about 20 cm by 30 cm and old newspapers.

We talked for a few minutes but since they seemed to know more about leaf printing than I did, I let them get on with it. I did one as well and realized that there is a certain amount of skill in getting sufficient paint on the leaf and then pressing with the hardboard to the right extent, if uniform results are wanted. I stopped them to point this out and then got them to try to produce uniform prints. (Was this a mistake? Was I inhibiting their experience of the medium?)

After about half an hour we compared results. Stephen had made a tree with additional brush work and Michaela had copied him. Ann and Christopher had made patterns using several colours. Melvyn had made a face out of overlapping prints. Tony's print was just a mess – he didn't seem to have much control over the materials, and a lot of paint went on him! Stephen and Ann are very articulate, but the others are quiet and Tony hardly said a word.

I suggested we make butterflies next using not more than two colours. Ann found a picture of a butterfly. To my surprise, Melvyn said, 'We ought to use plane tree leaves for making butterfly patterns'. He even knew where to get some plane tree leaves. (I didn't let him go because it was outside the school grounds. Could I have gone with him?)

2.40   During playtime I mounted the butterflies and Mr B found me some wall space.

3.00   Watched Mr B take a PE lesson. Warming up activities were based on pretending to be different kinds of animals. Four teams then worked with balls, hoops, ropes and skittles.

3.30   I read chapter 4 of the current book *Stig of the Dump*. Difficult because I don't know the story.

---

5   Drawing classroom plans

Drawing a simple plan of a classroom is a useful way of getting to know it, especially if care is taken to mark on the plan the location of the various teaching resources.

A scale of four feet to one inch is convenient in terms of most classrooms and of an A4 file page. Either draw the plan on $1/4$" graph paper or use a thick line grid under a plain sheet of paper to provide guide lines. In this way it should be possible to draw a reasonable sketch plan in about twenty minutes with freehand lines (use a thick fibre tip pen) and the help of a measuring tape.

The following conventions are suggested:

wall without window

wall with window in the top half

wall consisting entirely of window

carpet

table and chair

furniture which adults can see
over but not children

furniture which no one
can see over

bench with sink

A 'thick line grid' consists of a page
cross ruled with thick lines at $^1/_4$"
intervals like this:

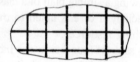

These conventions have been used in preparing the classroom plans of the
case studies of Part Two.

USE OF THE SCHOOL NOTEBOOK DURING STAGE TWO 'ONE GROUP' TEACHING

This section is concerned with the planning and evaluation of teaching
when a student is doing a limited amount of teaching only. It entails
detailed notes on what is intended and on how it went. The writing of such
notes is a very valuable activity because it focuses the mind systematically
on what is being done and trains a student-teacher to justify her classroom
actions. However it is also time consuming in its detail and becomes
impractical when a student is teaching a half-time load or more. At that
level of teaching, categorized here as stage four, a simplified form of
teaching notes is recommended; this is described later.

There are many ways of writing down teaching plans: a variety of headings may be used, such as aims, method, materials, stimulus, development, etc. After experience of several systems, and of the unstructured approach in which no system is offered to students, I have settled for the approach described here. This system arises from the description of teaching as an activity in which *resources* are used in *strategies* to achieve *objectives* based on the teacher's perceptions of children's educational *needs*. This terminology is explained in brief 10 on page 20. (See BASSEY, M. (1975) 'A paradigm for analysing teaching' *Education for Teaching* 98, 61–70.)

For each day a *forecast* is made of expected activities involving student and children. This gives for each activity an indication of the probable timing and, if possible, the names of the children likely to be involved. It includes a brief list of objectives for the activity, the main resources which will be required, and step-by-step notes of the intended strategy. After school an *evaluation* is written which briefly shows the extent to which the objectives seem to have been achieved, whether the resources and strategy were effective and includes any ideas for follow-up. The order in which objectives, resources and strategy are recorded is immaterial.

One point to be stressed is that the plan is a forecast and not a cast-iron mould. According to circumstances the forecasted activity may be abandoned or developed in a different way to that originally planned. Flexibility in teaching is vital, but this must not be an excuse for unpreparedness! If there is a change, this is described in the evaluation.

Group discussions in which intending infant teachers compare briefs 6 and 7, and intending junior teachers compare briefs 8 and 9, provide a useful introduction to the forecast/evaluation system based on objectives/resources/strategy. (These examples are invented – MB.) For infants 6 and for juniors 8, the briefs contain examples of students' teaching notes where the forecasts are inadequate and the evaluations trivial. The subsequent briefs, 7 for infants and 9 for juniors, use the same teachers' guidelines, but the forecasts and evaluations are written in terms of objectives, resources and strategy. Brief 10 describes these terms.

---

6 Infants, stage two teaching – extract from a notebook I

(These are a student's notes for a morning's work with mainly six children aged five to seven. The teacher (Miss T) has said, 'Make a sweetshop with pretend sweets which the children can use to practise some simple mathematics.' The student does not know the children yet.)

Tuesday 22 October Forecast

8.55   Registration etc. by Miss T.

9.10   Construct sweetshop and goods. Two children make sweetshop sign. Four make 'sweets' from pieces of wood and wrapping paper. (Put out large sheet of paper for sign and mix black paint. Put out small wood blocks for 'sweets'. Prepare paints – yellow, green and chocolate brown. Prepare wrapping paper.) They must clear up by playtime.

10.40   Playtime

11.00   Act a playlet using the shop.

11.25   The six children to write about what we have done.

11.40   Story for whole class: *Johnny Appleseed*

Evaluation

Making the sweetshop was much enjoyed and took all the morning up to story-time. No writing was done. I felt nervous when reading the story but nearly everybody listened.

---

7   Infants, stage two teaching – extract from a notebook II

(The situation is the same as in brief 6.)
Tuesday 22 October Forecast

8.55   Registration etc. by Miss T.

9.10–11.40   *SWEETSHOP*

Children   Six to be chosen by Miss T at registration.

Objectives

1   To make and use a mock-up of a sweetshop.

2   To promote: spoken language, social interaction, concepts of colour and size, use of money, and writing. (Which of these are important will depend upon which children I have.)

Resources

1   Corrugated paper, large boxes, small wooden blocks of different sizes, poster paints (thick), glue, wrapping paper, scissors, polystyrene tile, apple corer.

2   Box of pennies.

3   Writing paper and a scrapbook labelled 'Our sweetshop'; blank cards for words asked for by the children.

Strategy

8.30   1   Organize resources.

9.10   2   Group on carpet: 'This morning we are going to make a

16

sweetshop ... shut your eyes and imagine you are walking into a sweetshop ... now we will make a list of all the things that you saw ... what could you smell ... what other senses ... can you hear sweets ... what do they feel like?' Organize making activities through their choices: probably put children in pairs.

9.30   3   Making activities: shop sign (2 children, one older); cut peppermints from polystyrene foam; paint wood blocks — fudge, barley sugar, liquorice, chocolate; make a till out of a box; cut wrapping papers and wrap some sweets; count money.

10.30   4   Assemble shop. Tidy up.

10.40   5   Playtime. Put out writing materials and resources for the story.

11.00   6   Group on carpet. Each child reports on what he has done. Discussion of the playlet: shopkeeper, mother with child, two other customers, delivery man. Act.

11.25   7   Children write about what they have done during the morning; I will write words on cards when requested. Finished pieces to be glued in scrapbook.

11.40–12.00   *STORY: Johnny Appleseed*

Children — whole class

Objectives — language development and good listening

Resources — book, also an apple and knife

Strategy

1   Class on carpet. Cut apple. 'What are these? What colour are they? What are they for? ... This is a story about a man who planted the seeds of apples.'

2   Read story. Hold up pictures briefly.

3   Dismiss the class in terms of who can answer questions from the story and about apples ... core, stalk, pips, skin, colours ...

Evaluation

Sweetshop

1   Children: Susan, Mary, Darren, Angela, Michael, Robert

2   Timing went wrong; only 1 to 4 achieved; Miss T agrees to our continuing tomorrow. Children enthusiastic.

3   Stronger glue needed for fixing boxes together.

4   Michael and Robert took the lead in the making activities. Susan and Darren are very shy — they need more opportunities for self-expression. Angela and Darren muddle the colours. All except Michael and Mary need practice with the pennies.

Story

1 Went well; most children attentive, but not Willy nor Simon. (Must have them nearer to me tomorrow.)

2 Mary said, 'Can we plant some apple seeds?' Must ask Miss T if we can follow this up.

---

8 Juniors, stage two teaching – extract from a notebook I

(These are a student's notes for a one-hour class lesson with thirty-five children aged ten to eleven. The teacher (Mr R) has said, 'Talk with them about temperature and thermometers. Perhaps you could do an experiment and measure some temperatures. Next week I am going to show them how to convert Fahrenheit into Centigrade and vice-versa, so I want you to prepare the way for this. Keep them busy and I suggest you have them all doing the same work.')

Tuesday 22 October Forecast for a class lesson on Temperature

1 Draw up a list of everyday words that describe temperature.

2 Introduce idea of measuring temperature with a thermometer. Why do we need to measure it?

3 Tell story of Anders Celsius (1701–44) and Gabriel Fahrenheit (1686–1736).

4 Draw a thermometer on the chalkboard.

5 Put a fahrenheit and a centigrade thermometer into melting ice and then boiling water and have some children read the temperature.

6 Individual work for the children:

    (a) Draw up a table so that measurements in °C and °F can be compared.

    (b) List the words discussed earlier in terms of a temperature scale.

    (c) Make a drawing of a thermometer.

    (d) Make a graph of the measurements obtained in (a).

7 While they are working I will obtain some measurements from mixtures of hot and cold water – children can come out and read the temperatures.

Evaluation

This lesson went very well. I felt nervous at first. They were rather noisy when working on their own. Only a few made the graph.

---

9 Juniors, stage two teaching – extract from a notebook II

(The situation is the same as in brief 8)

Tuesday 22 October Forecast for a class lesson on Temperature
Objectives
1 To learn some simple facts about temperature and thermometers: what thermometers do, how they work, Centigrade and Fahrenheit scales, when these were invented.
2 To establish background knowledge for learning how to convert one scale into the other in the next lesson.
3 To use the subject matter as a vehicle for enquiry.

Strategy
10.40 1 Organize the resources during playtime. Draw outline of a thermometer and the results table on the chalkboard.
11.00 2 'This morning we are going to think about temperature. First, however, I want you all to turn your chairs round so that you are facing me ... Now, how hot do you feel? I will ask you in turn to say how hot or cold you feel ...' List these on chalkboard; expect – hot, cold, cool, warm, luke warm, freezing, boiling, (put in random order).
       3 'If we need to be more precise we use a thermometer ... when might we need a thermometer as an accurate measurement?' (Body temperature in illness; cooking temperature for cakes; when to put anti-freeze in car radiator ...) Describe thermometer.
       4 Talk about Anders Celsius (1701–44) and Gabriel Fahrenheit (1686–1736). Fahrenheit – German, born in Danzig, instrument maker, made mercury thermometers; lowest temperature he could achieve with ice and salt he called 0°F, his 100°F was body temperature – on this scale water boils at 212°F; later it was found more accurately that the average body temperature is between 98° and 99°F. Celsius – Swedish, born in Uppsala, astronomer; introduced the idea of 100 divisions between the melting point of ice and the boiling point of water on a mercury thermometer. He put the ice temperature as 100° and the boiling temperature as 0°; this was reversed after his death. Fahrenheit published in 1724; Celsius in 1742. How do scientists tell others about their ideas and discoveries? How do others know whether they are telling the truth? Both Fahrenheit and Celsius were Fellows of the Royal Society.
       5 Put a fahrenheit and a centigrade thermometer into melting ice and then boiling water and have some children read the temperature.
11.30 6 Individual work for the children:

(a) Make a copy of the table shown on the chalkboard.

(b) List the words used earlier in order of a temperature scale.

(c) Make a drawing of a thermometer. Six are available to be shared; care!

(d) For those who have finished all of the above a graph can be drawn – see me for this. I have an example on graph paper for them to copy from.

7 While the above is happening I will obtain temperature measurements of mixtures of hot and cold water using the two thermometers; children can come out to take the readings.

11.55 8 Ask someone to collect all papers for marking. Remember to tidy up floor and straighten furniture. Dismiss at noon.

Resources

1 Two thermometers (F and C) for reading from ice to boiling point; six others for drawing.

2 Three plastic cups, electric kettle (check classroom socket), thermos flask with crushed ice.

3 Writing paper, graph paper.

Evaluation

1 I felt that the basic facts (objective 1) went across. I will ask Mr R if I can spend a few minutes next week asking questions about these. The historical descriptions interested a number of children: especially Mary and Kalwent who want to do a 'topic' on Celsius and Fahrenheit – I must bring in my book for them. Tim and Felix might be persuaded to repeat the experiment with salt in the water – they showed some interest.

2 Very poor writing from Belinda, Felix, Peter and Janet. (Compared to other work of theirs.) Must see them tomorrow.

3 Objective 3 was difficult. I need to prepare more 'thinking' questions in advance.

4 Only John, Harpaveen, Tim and Elizabeth drew the graph and they needed much help from me. Perhaps this exercise was too difficult.

---

10 Forecasts and evaluations of teaching – Objectives, Strategies and Resources

This brief describes the forecast and evaluation system for planning and commenting on teaching recommended in this book. It provides a structure for thinking about the what, when, how and why of teaching. It is particularly appropriate for the early stages of learning to teach, when only a limited amount of teaching is being done by the student day by day. This approach is likely to be too time-consuming for anybody working to a full timetable, but it provides a training which leads to a simpler structure appropriate for such a timetable.

The system is based on this description of teaching:

> Teaching is an activity in which *resources* are used in *strategies* to achieve *objectives* based on the teacher's perceptions of children's educational *needs*.

Objectives are what you are trying to achieve as a teacher in terms of the children. (In this approach it embraces a range of concepts about intentions: aims, goals and purposes, etc.) Your objectives in setting up a teaching situation may be very general, for example, 'To develop the use of language', or may be quite specific, for example, 'To use the words "large" and "small" correctly in terms of a collection of boxes.' Some students find identifying objectives quite difficult; the best advice for these people is to keep asking the question 'What am I trying to achieve with and for the children?' Thus in brief 7 the answer is both making a sweetshop and trying to promote spoken language, social interaction, writing and several concepts. In brief 9, one objective is for the children to learn certain facts, and another objective is for them to gain experience of enquiry.

Resources are the things which are to be used in trying to achieve the objectives.

Strategy is the way in which you organize events in order to achieve the objectives. This extends from preparing the resources to evaluating the endpoints.

Before each day in school you are expected to write in your school notebook or file a *forecast* for each teaching activity for which you are responsible. These forecasts entail setting down the objectives of the activity, the resources to be used and the proposed strategy. In addition it may be appropriate to set down the brief given to you by your teacher and the names of the children involved if it is a group rather than the whole class. The forecast represents your prior intentions; it may be more appropriate in the event to organize a different activity or to change your strategy as the activity develops. If there is a thunderstorm it may be better to forget your planned work on Guy Fawkes and instead to write and paint in terms of the raw elements of nature. Flexibility and adaptability are important qualities in teachers.

The *evaluation* is written after school as a critical commentary on each activity and in particular on your view of the extent to which the objectives were achieved. It will be helpful to your future planning to make a brief reference to the effectiveness of the strategy and a note on how useful the resources were. If the activity is abandoned or modified this should be explained. Try to comment on the achievements of individual children and note any of their needs which could be met in the work of subsequent days. The forecast for the next round of activities for which you are responsible should incorporate points made in the previous evaluation.

Keep your notebook as tidy as practical with date, margin and ruled line between days. Remember that it is an 'open' book for your tutor, teacher and headteacher.

GROUP PLANNING EXERCISES FOR STAGE TWO

Some students adopt the objectives-resources-strategy system easily, others find it takes time and practice to accommodate their thinking pattern to this approach. In my experience, about one student in ten finds that it is of no help to her and that she needs to plan her teaching in a less structured way.

The activities suggested in the next two briefs are planning exercises for groups of three or four students. The interaction in a group helps to develop the concepts of objectives, resources and strategy, particularly if a tutor is available for consultation.

11   Planning work for a group of infants

This is an activity to carry out in groups of three or four; it is an opportunity to practise writing a teaching forecast, using the objectives-resources-strategy system.

You are to simulate the work of a student who is associated with a vertically grouped infant class.

The teacher has asked you to work with eight children tomorrow morning: Angela, Fraser, Gary, John, Michelle, Sharon, Peter and Tracy. A milkman is to visit the class early in the morning to describe his work to the children and to answer their questions; the teacher will be responsible for this part. After the milkman has left you are to organize your eight children in making a collage of the milkman and in painting pictures of him at work. Some writing is also expected from these children: they are in the middle age range and can write on their own if you supply them with words – except for Peter and John who are only at the stage of copying underneath the teacher's writing. Angela is a very withdrawn child who hardly ever speaks; Michelle is inclined to be dominant in any group – yesterday she had a fight with Gary over a painting.

Prepare a forecast for the period after playtime – 10.45 to 12 noon.

12 Planning a lesson for a junior class

This is an activity to carry out in groups of three or four; it is an opportunity to practise writing a teaching forecast using the objectives-resources-strategy system.

You are to simulate the work of a student who is associated with a third year junior class of thirty-five children.

The teacher has asked you to give a forty-five minute lesson to the whole class on the theme 'Inventing machines to get people out of bed in the morning.' (Are you familiar with Edward de Bono's work?)

The teacher suggests that you have a discussion followed by individual work by the children and eventually display the results on the wall.

The children sitting on table 4 find difficulty with writing and need considerable help.

Prepare a forecast for the lesson.

USE OF THE SCHOOL NOTEBOOK DURING STAGE THREE 'MORE THAN ONE GROUP' TEACHING

The transition from Stage two to Stage three requires a major accommodation in teaching style. In Stage two the student-teacher is interacting with her group or class all the time: talking to them, listening, directly supervising their work. But in Stage three, by definition she has more than one group in action for at least part of the time, and this means that she can only physically be with one group at a time. Thus the other group or groups need to have been given work that they can get on with in relative isolation.

Stage three requires more planning than Stage two, and an important aspect of that planning is that the student-teacher needs to work out a forecast for sharing her time between the various groups.

One criterion of readiness to move on to Stage three is obviously competence in the classroom, but another, which may not be so obvious, is the ability to write forecasts and evaluations quickly and effectively. Until a student-teacher is skilful at using her notebook as a basic tool for planning her teaching, it is unwise to burden her with the demands of Stage three. An indication of whether she is ready to move on to Stage three is the amount of time it takes her to keep the notebook up-to-date. Stage three planning requires more writing than Stage two, but the guideline of not more than one hour a day is still appropriate – for the writing and related thinking about teaching.

The following brief gives an example of a student's notes for a one-hour lesson with first-year juniors, where three groups are to be operating at one time. It is worth making the point that at this stage of a student's development it would be unreasonable to expect any other teaching from the student during the day. The rest of the day should be spent on assisting teacher in activities which demand no preparation from the student.

The brief might take a student a couple of hours to prepare, but since it ntains work for three groups and through rotation will be used three nes, it is within the above guideline for preparation time, allowing for out twenty minutes for making evaluative comments after each lesson.

3 Stage three teaching – extract from a notebook

These are notes in preparation for a seventy-five minute lesson with a class of thirty first-year junior children who are organized into three mixed-ability groups of ten children. Each group occupies a set of tables pushed together. The student-teacher knows all of the children and they are used to doing rotating group-work. The class teacher started a topic on Spring time a few days back and has asked the student to organize group work in mathematics, writing and art work on this theme. The lesson is to be repeated on a rotating basis on the following days.)

Tuesday 23 March Forecast for group work from 10.45 to 12 noon
RED GROUP
Objective
To reinforce last week's work on block graphs in terms of making and understanding them.

Resources
1 spring flowers in a bowl
2 squared paper
3 my work cards
4 pencils, crayons, rulers.

Strategy
1 Tell children to make a list in their books of flowers in the vase and to put the number of each kind. Work cards for Ann, Michael and Peter; the rest should be able to do it without help. When done they can draw pictures in $\frac{1}{2}$" squares at top of sheet of squared paper as key to graph. Stress neatness. Remind about Mr R's rule about rubbers.
2 Children draw block graphs as last week – picture in each square. Crayon in. Check on A, M and P. Hands up when finished.
3 Check graphs as hands go up; issue work cards individually; explain if necessary. Hands up when finished so that I can mark each in turn.

There are six work cards (three copies of each) – expect most children to do two or three of these.

4 Last fifteen minutes must work on their own. Read story books if necessary.

YELLOW GROUP

Objective

To express ideas in written and spoken language.

Resources

1 Cassette tape of me reading three poems about spring flowers. (five mins)
2 My work cards.

Strategy

1 Children to listen to tape. Tell them to hear it twice and second time to choose some interesting words which they might use themselves. (Put Steven in charge of tape recorder).
2 Discussion with me about the words they have chosen. Write difficult ones on work cards. Tell them to write either a poem or a story about spring flowers; discuss ideas as a group with me. Hands up if they want words, but encourage them to use the class dictionaries. Special work card for Belinda.
3 Leave them to work on their own – minimum supervision.
4 At 11.45 I will read their writings aloud to the group and discuss with them.

BLUE GROUP

Objective

To develop accurate observation and recording using pencil, paint and black outlining pen.

Resources

1 daffodils and bluebells
2 paints (made up), brushes, water pots, pencils, black felt pens
3 paper and newspaper.

Strategy

1 Children to cover tables with newspaper, put out paints and water pots etc., and then to look carefully at the flowers but not to start work till I join them.
2 Discuss shapes of the flowers with the children. Demonstrate one drawing – stress big pictures that fill the sheet. Tell them to draw pencil

25

outlines, paint, and – when the paint is dry – outline in black with felt pen. Each child can do one picture of a daffodil and one of bluebell. Stress good observation. Put names on sheets.

3 Leave them to work on their own – minimum supervision, but be ready to discipline John if he is difficult.

4 At 11.45 children to clear away. They can put their pictures on the pinboard over the radiator. If time to spare they may read their story books.

My strategy

10.30 Playtime. Put out resources for red and yellow group. Check that blue group's resources are in the cupboard.

10.45 Announce group work; stress that expect everybody to be busy and to work neatly. Give initial instructions to yellow and blue group. Let them start.

10.50 Work with red group (1): five mins.

10.55 Blue group (2): five mins.

11.00 Yellow group (2): ten mins.

11.10 General supervision – mainly red and yellow groups. Make tick list notes on their work. ('Tick lists' are described in brief 23 on page 41.)

11.45 Announcements for red group (4) and blue group (4).

11.46 Work with yellow group (4); make tick list notes: twelve mins.

11.58 Everything away; tidy up if necessary; if time refer to blue group's paintings; dismiss class.

CHILDREN'S EDUCATIONAL NEEDS AND TEACHERS' OBJECTIVES

During Stage two and Stage three, students should be encouraged to refer to individual children in the evaluations of school work, and to write prescriptions for future activity rather than factual descriptions of what has happened. When working with small numbers of children this is a relatively simple task, but as a student comes to work with more children, she inevitably finds increasing difficulty in thinking positively about all of them.

The following approach to this problem develops from the description of teaching used earlier: teaching is an activity in which resources are used in strategies to achieve *objectives based on the teacher's perceptions of children's educational needs*. The approach is based on two questions:

What are the educational needs of the children as a whole?

Which of these are especially important for each individual child now?

With this analysis it is possible to move from a general statement of the educational needs of the class, as perceived by the student-teacher, to a short list of important objectives for each child in the immediate future.

The following briefs give suggestions for carrying out this analysis. This thinking is an important preparation for Stage four teaching.

---

14 Children's educational needs in general

Educational needs include what the individual child needs for himself and what he needs as a member of society. Some needs are the desires of the child himself; some are the desires of others for him. Some needs are of the present and others are of the future.

Needs can be expressed in many different ways. Some teachers use the PIES mnemonic: that children have *p*hysical, *i*ntellectual, *e*motional, and *s*ocial needs. In this brief it is recommended that you analyse needs in rather more detail.

The following list of educational needs of young children illustrates the level of detail which is needed for the analytical exercise of brief 15.

1   The need for personal security, happiness and success.
2   The need to make personal decisions and so to become less dependent upon others.
3   The need to interact with other people cooperatively.
4   The need (a) to understand the routine of the classroom, and (b) to acquire positive attitudes towards learning.
5   The need to develop the use of language through the skills of talking and listening.
6   The need to develop the use of language through the skills of reading and writing.
7   The need to acquire and to use mathematical concepts and to develop the ability to reason logically.
8   The need to develop the coordination of brain and body.
9   The need to express creative ideas.
10 The need to engage in enquiry.
11 The need to develop aesthetic sensitivity and to acquire aesthetic values.
12 The need to develop moral sensitivity and to acquire moral values.
13 The need to acquire everyday knowledge.
14 The need to understand oneself and one's environment.

Activity

Draw up your list of educational needs of the children in your class. For convenience, try to keep the list to between eight and twenty items. If the above list exactly fits your perceptions use it as your list, or modify it according to your own thinking. But avoid using phrases which are not intelligible to you in the context of your classroom. Give each item in your list a number.

15 Individual children's educational needs

This activity uses the list of children's educational needs drawn up as suggested in the previous brief.

Make a list of about half a dozen children whom you know well. Against the name of each child write down the reference numbers of three items from your list of needs, which you feel to be *the most important needs for him or her during the next few weeks of school work.*

Your list might look like this:

John Brown	1	3	5
Peter Clark	6	7	13
Susan Dodd	1	3	4

In some cases it may be that only one or two needs seem paramount, while in others you may feel the obligation to put down more than three. Again you may feel that against each child you should enter the total list of needs because as a class teacher you would seek to be 'all things to all men'. Avoid this latter view; this exercise is about priorities in the classroom and it is important as a teacher to be able to identify immediate needs.

Sometimes it is more appropriate to enlarge on this exercise by writing notes in addition. For example:

Mary Evans	6	9	10	Her writing is competent but unimaginative.
Carol Hughes	7	2	5	She doesn't understand the current work on area; she needs encouraging to speak up for herself.
Paul McKenzie	10	13	14	Basic skills good but he never asks questions.
Kevin Roberts	8	5	3	Clumsy and physically awkward. Needs practice – ball catching, carrying water jug, balancing.

These examples show how the general list of needs can be applied to individuals and then focused on specific and immediate needs. Each of the above comments could lead to action in the classroom. Mary could work in a small group on de Bono's 'Think-Link' cards; Carol might receive several 'three-minute-sessions' of individual attention; Paul could be given regular exercises of writing lists of questions about objects; Kevin might be paired with someone who regularly helped him carry out the physical exercises suggested.

ASCERTAINING CHILDREN'S NEEDS

The activities of briefs 14 and 15, if carefully undertaken and discussed in detail, should provide students with a simple approach to defining objectives for the whole class, long term, and for individual children, short term. This illustrates the way in which in the objectives/resources/strategy system for describing teaching and the educational needs of children, as perceived by their teacher, are the raw materials from which she forms her objectives for them. It is worth making the point that any teacher can expect that her general list of perceived needs will change slightly from time to time, influenced by her experience of children, discussion with colleagues and her reading.

Brief 16 suggests a way in which a student preparing for a school practice at stage four, 'most of the children most of the time', can so structure her initial visits to the classroom that she begins to know the children in terms of their educational needs.

16 Classroom observation of children in small groups

Before you engage in Stage four teaching – 'most of the children for most of the time' – it is to everybody's advantage for you to know the children individually. If you are to teach them effectively you need to know not only their names, but something of their educational needs. These notes suggest a means by which you can meet the children and learn sufficient about them to make a first assessment of their educational needs using the approach recommended in brief 15.

The idea is that you meet the class in groups of say eight junior children for an hour or of four infant children for half an hour. If possible this should be outside the classroom – in a cloakroom, corridor or spare room if there is one.

It is probably best if you ask your teacher to set it up by saying to the class something like:

In a few weeks time Miss A is going to be teaching you for most of the time in place of me. So that you can get to know her, and so that she can know what your best work is like, she is going to meet you in small groups. When your turn comes, take your maths book, your topic book and ... and go with Miss A to the far end of the corridor. Now we will start with Susan, John ...

Start with a group discussion. This could be about an object which you have brought with you (especially for younger children) or on a recent class activity or about the locality. Then set a piece of writing – or a drawing for those who can't yet write: unless it seems banal, a piece of personal writing is both easy for the children and useful to you – a description of self and of home, parents, friends, interests. While the writing is in progress talk to each child in turn and examine his books. Make quick written notes on his level of competence in mathematics, written work, speech, etc. and of any obvious behavioural characteristics. Watch the timing of each of these interviews! Perhaps end up by telling them something about yourself.

Afterwards try to make a first assessment of their educational needs.

PATTERNS OF CLASSROOM AND TEAM TEACHING ORGANIZATION

One of the problems of studying primary schools is that there is not a universal language to describe patterns of teaching organization.

The next two briefs describe a system that I have developed, which focuses on children's activity in terms of periods of time, rather than on the overall organization. The system for describing classroom teaching can be linked to that for describing team teaching and examples of this are given in the case studies of Part Two.

Brief 17 describes four common patterns of classroom organization and brief 18 sets out a way of describing team teaching units. Brief 19 suggests a method of observation which can be useful for a student about to move into Stage four teaching.

I have deliberately omitted the term 'integrated day' from the next two briefs because it is variously used to describe the integration of time, space, activity, curriculum and staff. Patterns 3 and 4 of brief 17 and patterns C, D and E of brief 18 are examples of activities which some would call 'integrated'. Case study 2 (page 111) is a detailed study of one interpretation of the 'integrated day'.

17 Four patterns of classroom organization

There are four major patterns of classroom organization used by primary school teachers as ways of arranging the activity of their children. It is usual to find that two or three of these are in regular use at different times in the day, or week, and in some classrooms all four are used. These occur in both infant and junior schools.

Pattern 1: Classwork in one subject
Periods of time *when the attention of the class is on the same work, either individually or collectively.* For example: teacher gives class instruction on mathematics; teacher reads story; all children do sums individually from blackboard or from workbooks; all children paint; all children read silently; all children write stories.

Pattern 2: Groupwork in one subject
Periods of time *when only one subject is in progress, but different groups are engaged in different aspects of it, either individually or collectively within groups.* For example, groupwork in mathematics: one group is working individually on sums from their textbooks, a second group is working collectively in measuring the room, a third group is engaged on work cards on shape individually, and a fourth group is doing practical work with the teacher on capacity.

Pattern 3: Groupwork in several subjects
Periods of time *when different groups are engaged in different subjects.* For example: the red group is doing mathematics individually, the blue group is writing stories, the yellow group is working at 'topic' and the green group is engaged in painting or clay work.

Pattern 4: Individual work in several subjects
Periods of time *when children are engaged in individual studies in different subjects and without any regular grouping.* For example: some children are doing mathematics, some are writing stories, some are working at 'topic' and others are painting or doing craft work; they are engaged in these activities either by their own choice or because the teacher so directed them. This pattern differs from Pattern 3 because on another day the sets of children doing mathematics, writing, 'topic' and art work would be different because different individual decisions would be made.

A useful way of getting to grips with the organization of a particular class is to prepare a weekly timetable in terms of the different patterns in use. Once this is clear a number of questions come to the fore. Do the children sit in particular places? How are the places arranged? What is the basis of grouping? Do the groups rotate? Are there clear expectations by the teacher on what work shall be done in Pattern 4? Are the children set assignments; do they use job cards? Some of these questions are suggested in Part Two.

18 Five patterns of team teaching organization

There seem to be five major patterns of organization used by primary school teachers in open-plan team teaching situations. In any one school several of these will be in use. They are found in both infant and junior schools.

Pattern A: Assemblies
Periods of time *when all members of a unit* (school, wing, division, area, etc.) *come together,* i.e. all of the groups which are the responsibility of the team of teachers. (Although assemblies are a feature of all schools, in team teaching situations they may be used for instructional purposes, which is less usual in schools organized on a class basis.)

Pattern B: Base groupwork
Periods of time *when the children whose names are on one attendance register stay together.* (These may be called 'home' groups or 'register' groups, etc.)

Pattern C: Team work – fixed groups
Periods of time *when the base groups have subdivided and recombined into groupings which have the same fixed membership each time they form.* For example: each base group may divide into 'reds', 'blues' and 'greens' and all the 'reds' come together to do mathematics, all the 'blues' do writing and all the 'greens' do creative work. Each is taught by one member of the team.

Pattern D: Team work – variable groups
Periods of time *when the base groups have subdivided and recombined into groupings which have a variable membership each time they form.* For example: each base group divides up according to either the children's own choices or the teacher's directions so that children who are to do mathematics go to the mathematics area, those who are to do writing go to the writing area and those who are to do creative work go to that area. Each group is taught by one member of the team. On another day the sets of children would be different because different individual decisions would have been made.

Pattern E: Individual work on assignments
Periods of time *when children are engaged in individual studies which have been assigned to them, in different subjects, and when there is no regular grouping of children.*

19   Classroom observation of a teacher

1   Observation of an experienced teacher working with her class is a valuable part of teacher training. But you must realize that everybody feels self-conscious on being observed and so it needs to be arranged with great sensitivity and awareness. Strict adherence to the following rules is recommended:

   (i)   That the teacher is only observed in the way to be described if she agrees.
   (ii)   That the observation notes are purely descriptive and not evaluative.
   (iii) That the notes are made available to the teacher for her perusal.
   (iv)   That the notes are not shown to anyone other than your tutor unless the teacher gives her permission.

2   Much of the success of teaching in primary schools depends upon organization and management. Having had some experience of teaching you should be ready to pick out significant points of organization and management in the work of the teacher to be observed. How does she talk to the children; are there special phrases which they mutually understand? How does she initiate work? How does she supervise several groups at a time? How does the pattern of work change for the children? How does the teacher control the children; what sanctions does she use? How does she encourage them?

3   The observation procedure is to make notes of significant events as they occur throughout one day. This entails taking a passive role in the classroom and writing in notebook or on a clip board. It is as well if your teacher explains to the children what is happening. For example: 'Today Miss A is going to be writing about what we are doing. So I want you to try to remember not to ask her to help you – just for today. She may come and ask you what you are doing and then I hope you will tell her.'

4   The following extract from a notebook is of observation in an infant classroom:

   8.30   Miss B arrives in the classroom and organizes materials for the morning.
   8.45   Door opened. During next ten minutes children come in, some with mothers, take coats off, talk to Miss B, look at the

display of yellow things that has just been put up, sit on carpet.

9.02   Miss B sits in chair by carpet and takes register and dinner money. A few number questions are discussed and also today's weather.

9.15   Miss B talks with the children about yellow objects using items from the display. There is great excitement when she lifts a yellow box to reveal a yellow budgerigar in a cage; the bird sings ... Several children kneel; 'No. On your bottoms, please.' One child hits another; 'Simon. Come and sit by me.'

9.22   Miss B stands up and organizes the work for the rest of the morning. The red group are to go to the writing area to write about something yellow. The blue group are to do number work; 'I want the older children to be sure to do three cards today. Hands up the older children in the blue group. That's right.' The green group are to choose between clay, painting and the Wendy corner: 'Remember, not more than four in any corner. And if you are painting, what must you wear? That's right.' All the children stay sitting on the carpet while Miss B gives these instructions. (Three minutes.)

9.25   'Now. Off you go. Everybody busy please.' Children move quickly. The green group seem to divide into fours without fuss. Miss B goes to the writing area and gathers the children round her. There is a brief discussion and she writes some words on a sheet for them to use.

9.31   'The people in the number area are getting too noisy. I will come and help you soon.'

9.32   Observer visits number area. Mark, John, Susy, Tom: sorting coloured objects. Mary, James, Peter: using large dominoes. Keith, Samantha, Robert, Elaine: work cards on number bonds.

9.35   Miss B joins number group and talks to each child in turn.

5   Endeavour to write up the notes on the same day and to discuss them with your teacher on the following day if possible, while the events are still fresh in your mind. Examples of this kind of study are included in the case studies of Part Two.

SCHOOL NOTEBOOKS FOR STAGE FOUR: 'MOST OF THE CHILDREN MOST OF THE TIME'

After working with small groups of children or with the whole class for short periods, comes the time to practise teaching most of the children for most of the time. This is the common pattern for a final teaching practice and may last for six to twelve weeks. The class teacher usually has minimal contact with the class and either works with other children or withdraws from her own class such children as need special help and who can profit from her individual attention. It is also common for students on a first or second teaching practice to spend a few days at the end of the practice working at this stage.

The following briefs are intended to promote discussion of the notes and records which it is helpful for a student-teacher at this stage to keep. After a full day of working in school, from say 8.30 a.m. to 4.30 p.m., plus travelling, most people are tired. It is therefore important to ensure that the writing of records for the day and of making a forecast for the next day is so organized that it is not overtaxing. The guideline suggested earlier of not more than one hour to be spent on planning and writing notes per day is reiterated. Even so it is likely that further time will be needed for finding teaching resources and for writing work cards etc.

One of the important features of Stage four is that students need to find a balance between curriculum plans designed for the class as a whole and the needs of individual children. Both are discussed in the briefs.

The briefs assume that students are placed in class teaching situations and not team teaching ones. I believe that it is a mistake to place a student for a final practice into a team situation. My reason is that for her to try to get to know about a hundred children so that she can make educational prescriptions for their work is virtually an impossible task. It can be done for a class – along the lines suggested in Brief 16 – but larger numbers prevent the student from learning to balance the demands of a curriculum with the needs of individuals. Experience of team teaching is valuable, particularly because it encourages students to work and cooperate with other adults, but it is inappropriate for a final teaching practice. These remarks of course assume that a college has the opportunity of placing its students in either kind of situation; this is not the case everywhere.

---

20 School notebooks – stage four teaching: I

Stage four entails teaching most of the children for most of the time, and this requires several kinds of notes and records. It may be best to use several notebooks rather than put everything into one book. As a progression from the ideas developed earlier it is suggested that the following series of notes are required for Stage four work in school.

(i)   A description of the school, classroom, curriculum and overall organization. See brief 3.
(ii) An overall forecast for the teaching practice period. It is useful if this is related to the existing curriculum and organization of the class's own teacher. See brief 21.
(iii) Records of individual children. See brief 22.
(iv) Daily record book (or 'tick' book). See brief 23.
(v)   Curriculum forecasts (or schemes of work). See brief 24.
(vi) Daily forecasts and general evaluations. See brief 25.

Most of the examples given in the briefs are based on infant work, but the ideas are equally applicable to juniors.

There are obviously many ways in which a teaching practice can be planned and evaluated. The suggestions made in these briefs may or may not be the appropriate ways for you, but at least they should stimulate your own ideas on what notes you will require.

The way in which these link together is shown in Figure 1 on p. 37. First of all a description of school, classroom, curriculum and existing pattern of organization is made. This leads to the preparation of an overall forecast for the teaching practice. In turn, the overall forecast leads to forecasts for each of the curriculum areas in which the children are to be taught – language, mathematics, themes or topics, art and craft, physical education, music, etc. Also before the practice, records of individual children are started and the forecast for day 1 is prepared. During day 1, a tick record is kept and that evening an evaluation of the day's work is made. Also on the evening of day 1, the forecast for day 2 is prepared and the arrows in the diagram show how this forecast is strongly influenced by the curriculum forecasts made before the practice started, and is also influenced by what happened on day 1 (as shown by the tick book and the end-of-the-day evaluation) and by the records of individual children.

It is worth adding a note about the relevance of this to Stage five – 'Full-time teaching – just surviving'. If as a student you kept a school notebook, with forecasts and evaluations, just because your tutor required it, then it is likely that as a probationary teacher you will do little planning on paper – unless your head requires it. On the other hand, if you have followed through the sequence and development of ideas put forward in this book, it is likely that you will find the system summarized in this brief to be a useful basis for classroom planning in the early years of your teaching. A recommended way of working for probationary teachers is to divide the

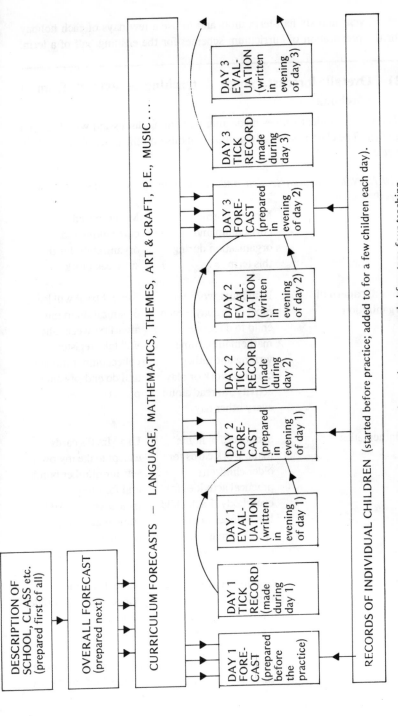

Figure 1. Relationship between the various forecasts and records recommended for stage four teaching

DESCRIPTION OF SCHOOL, CLASS etc. (prepared first of all)

OVERALL FORECAST (prepared next)

CURRICULUM FORECASTS — LANGUAGE, MATHEMATICS, THEMES, ART & CRAFT, P.E., MUSIC....

DAY 1 FORE-CAST (prepared before the practice)

DAY 1 TICK RECORD (made during day 1)

DAY 1 EVAL-UATION (written in evening of day 1)

DAY 2 FORE-CAST (prepared in evening of day 1)

DAY 2 TICK RECORD (made during day 2)

DAY 2 EVAL-UATION (written in evening of day 2)

DAY 3 FORE-CAST (prepared in evening of day 2)

DAY 3 TICK RECORD (made during day 3)

DAY 3 EVAL-UATION (written in evening of day 3)

RECORDS OF INDIVIDUAL CHILDREN (started before practice; added to for a few children each day).

school year into six half-term units and to use a few days of each holiday for the preparation of curriculum schemes for the ensuing half of a term.

21 Overall forecast, stage 4 teaching – extract from a notebook

(These are a student's notes made after a planning discussion with the class teacher. The class is vertically grouped infants and the practice will last six weeks.)

7.10.76 Notes on organization and curriculum following discussion with Mrs P

	Mrs P's normal curriculum and organization during this term	My proposed curriculum and organization for the six-week block
Overall pattern of organization	Individual work for most of the day – each child to do some mathematics, some writing and either creative work or play activity; to read aloud every other day.	Same. Mrs P will leave organization to me after first week. She will take register, collect dinner money and do end-of-school prayers.
Mathematics	Sequences of home-made work cards for older children; practical activities for everybody. Each child has number book which is marked regularly in class.	Use Mrs P's cards except make my own sets for number bonds and for linear measurement. Add some practical activities.
Reading	Colour coded system based on Ladybird, Kathy and Mark, and Through the Rainbow.	Same. Introduce Nippers series for older children.
Story	Fifteen min at end of each day; alternately	Same pattern: choose stories for four days a

	for younger and older children.	week; Mrs P to read once a week.
Topic	Major topic every half term and two or three minor ones. At present: Birds and also Red Things and Mirrors. Each child has writing book (marked in class)	Choose major topic and three minor ones. Include one coach visit.
Art and craft	Painting, clay work, collage.	Continue these but add tie and dye and at some stage replace collage with box work.
Play activities	Big bricks, little bricks, dressing up materials, home corner, dry sand, water trough, woodwork bench.	Remove water trough and woodwork bench. Continue others. Introduce new dressing up materials and refurnish home corner. Change dry sand to wet.
Physical education	Floorwork and small apparatus.	Introduce some creative dance.

22 Records of individual children

The children in your class will be at different stages in their development, will be changing at different rates and will have different educational needs. For these reasons individual records are required so that as a teacher you can reflect on each child and attempt to tailor your curriculum plans to individual requirements.

Getting to know the educational characteristics of about thirty-five children in the few weeks of a block teaching practice is not easy and this emphasizes the value of preliminary visits, in which you meet the children in small groups, as suggested in brief 16.

It is suggested that you keep a loose-leaf file with one page per child and with the piece of personal writing or drawing produced by each child during your preliminary visits inserted opposite your notes on him. Short entries can be made from time to time as significant events occur.

If you have adopted the suggestion of brief 14 and drawn up a list of the children's educational needs, it will be helpful to glue this as a fold-out sheet to the inside cover of the notebook so that you can refer to it regularly.

Some entries will inevitably be only descriptive, but as far as possible try to make prescriptive points, i.e. your ideas on what activities the child should engage in, or on what behaviour you should reinforce, so as to promote his educational development.

Two examples may provide a focus for discussion: one infant and one junior.

SIMON BROWN   age 6.2

3.11.76   Curly fair hair, blue eyes.

5.11.76   Sister in the juniors; he is friendly with Peter Mann.

10.11.76* My assessment of his major needs: 2, 5, 6.
           Reading: stage 2
           Writing: stage 1
           Number: stage 2
           Very quiet and shy.

19.11.76   Talked hesitatingly to class about his fire-engine collage: first time! Must encourage him to talk in small groups.

30.11.76   Some progress in coming out of his shell – make him milk monitor next week with Peter Mann.

8.12.76   Writing has doubled in volume. Stage 2. Find something of his to display on wall.

(* This was the preliminary visit when I talked to his group.)

A point for discussion is whether individual records should contain items such as: 'parents divorced, lives with step-mother', 'eldest of five, often tired because of housework', 'IQ 95', 'parents very anxious for her success', 'father is university lecturer'. Do these descriptions affect your expectations of what the child can achieve? If 'yes', is it not better to try to ignore these points, to have high expectations for every child, and to make your prescriptions in terms of each child's classroom performance?

The references to stages in writing, reading and number work are based on the student's concepts of development in these areas of the curriculum.

JOANNA SMITH   age 9.7
4.11.76   Brown hair, brown eyes, freckly face.
10.11.76* Writing: plenty of it but help needed with punctuation and spelling of some simple words.
           Reading aloud: fluent.
           Mathematics: group 3; on Fletcher II book 6 section 8; she said, 'I don't like decimals'.
           My assessment of her major needs at present: 4b, 10, 2.
17.11.76   Seems to be idling in class – must arouse her interest. Try colour supplement on netball as starting point for an assignment.
1.12.76   Still idling. Must talk with her and try to find some starting points. Then insist on good work.
6.12.76   Assignment time to be spent on *Goldfish*: her choice. Watch her!

(* This was the preliminary visit when I talked to her group.)

---

23   Daily records – three way tick book

In addition to a personal record for each child it can be helpful to keep a check list or 'tick book' for day-by-day activity. This is one way of ensuring that you are regularly aware of each individual member of the class; it is particularly useful if the class is organized mainly in Pattern 2, 3 or 4.

It is suggested that instead of using a single tick, you adopt the following three tick system. This not only records the fact that a child has done a piece of work, but also gives your prescription for his next piece of work, viz:

 the child should continue with work at his present level in order to reinforce present learnings;

 the child is in need of help – he is experiencing difficulty in what he is doing at present;

 the child is ready to advance to the next stage of work and may become bored unless he is moved on soon.

41

The ability on your part to use these ticks requires your having a stage-by-stage sense of the development of the child's learning in the area of the curriculum under study.

The following is an example of an infant teacher's tick book. Note that points of concern are entered on one side. The book is long and thin, with the names of the class down the left hand side of the cover and some headings on the cover at the top. The inserted pages are smaller and are ruled. One double page is used per day.

	WRITING	NUMBER	READING ALOUD	PARTICULAR POINTS
DAY and DATE	1 Nov : Mon			
John Brown	✗	✓		writing in columns
Mary Cook	✓	✓	✓	
Peter Dunn	✓			no number work
Penelope Fox	✓	✓	✓	
Darryl Ginn	✓	✓		
Sugit Hogal	✓	✓	✓	move onto 10-20

24 Curriculum forecast for 6 weeks' stage 4 teaching – extract from a notebook

(This relates to the vertically grouped infant class referred to in Brief 21.)

Overall pattern of organization on a typical day: 36 children

9.00 Sit on mat – register, dinners, discussion.
9.10 School assembly.
9.30 Return to classroom – sit on mat – instructions for period 1.
9.35 Activity period 1 – individual work mainly. (Sometimes discussion for about fifteen minutes to initiate new work.) Milk after 10.00.

10.25	Tidy up and then sit on mat.
10.30	Playtime.
10.50	Return to classroom – sit on mat – instructions for period 2.
10.55	Activity period 2 – individual work Tuesday and Thursday; on Monday, Wednesday, Friday – PE in hall until 11.25, then class discussion on mat.
11.45	Tidy up.
11.50	Sit on mat – class discussion or singing. Wash hands/toilet.
12.00	Dinner time (usually twelve non-diners).
1.30	Sit on mat – register – instructions for period 3.
1.35	Activity period 3 – individual work mainly. (Sometimes fifteen minutes discussion.)
2.25	Tidy up.
2.30	Playtime.
2.50	Return to classroom – sit on mat – discussion. Complete tidying as necessary – put chairs up. Story.
3.25	Prayers.
3.30	Children leave.

Mathematics

General context: Mrs P has a detailed scheme for children to progress through over the two to three years. Each child is expected to do some mathematics every day, which is marked in class. See list of children (details omitted – MB.)

(a) *NUMBER BONDS*

Context: twelve children (John, Peter, Mary ...) can count up to twenty and beyond and should be ready for number bond work up to twenty.

Objectives: for the children:
To reinforce counting up to twenty and the writing of these numbers.
To use a strip number chart one to twenty for adds and take-aways.
Through regular use to memorise the number bonds up to ten.
Through occasional use to become familiar with the number bonds up to twenty (treating ten, eleven to... as numbers with names and ignoring place value at this stage).

Strategy
Work cards to be copied into their number books:

yellow cards: counting practice
orange cards: strip number chart practice

red cards: number bonds through objects
brown cards: number bonds through symbols.

Each child initially to do one each of yellow, orange and red cards per day – more later as I assess their ability.
Introduce these cards as a group lesson.
Evaluate through my tick book.

Resources
Work cards, counting objects, strip number charts, display number chart.

  (b) *LINEAR MEASUREMENT*

  (c) *MRS P'S WORK CARDS*
      Context: the older children are working through a detailed scheme based on Fletcher's Mathematics. I shall mark their books regularly and keep a note of their progress through my tick book.

  (d) *COUNTING AND SORTING (Details have been omitted – MB.)*

Talking
Objectives
For all children to develop their spoken language skills as a tool for thinking and learning across the curriculum.
For all children to use language appropriately in a variety of situations.
For Keith and Darryl: to start talking in the classroom (i) with other children and (ii) with me.

Strategies
(i) Child-child discussion; (ii) Child-teacher discussion; (iii) Children-teacher discussion.
For Keith and Darryl: groups to be so structured as to encourage (i) and special attention by me to make the opportunity of (ii) at least once a day. (Enter in tick book for these two boys.)

Writing
Context: Every child is expected to do some writing every day. This arises either from the topics in hand or from the story, news, or any other casual stimulus. Children at three stages. (Details omitted – MB.)

Objectives
For each child to learn the skills of writing according to his stage of development.
For the children to gain pleasure from creative expression.

Strategies
Each child to write and to bring his daily work to me when completed for marking. Use tick book to evaluate. Stimulus from topic etc.

Stage (a) Child draws picture, I write description as dictated by child, child either traces on top of or copies my writing, completes work by reading it to me.

Stage (b) Sentence book: I write at child's dictation in his sentence book, he copies into his writing book, and then comes and reads it back to me.

Stage (c) Alphabet books: children find their own words from their alphabet books and from wall displays, picture dictionaries etc. I write words in the alphabet books on request – but encourage the children to help each other.

Flash cards work: for stage (a) names; for stage (b) other words.

(Choose week by week according to needs of children.)

Display some writing regularly on the wall.

Letter forming practice for stage (c) children.

Reading

Context: Every child has a reading book and is heard once every two days for two to three minutes. There is a colour system, devised by Mrs P, using Ladybird, Kathy and Mark and Through the Rainbow. Each child has a book marker on which is written the last page number which he has successfully read aloud. When a book is complete he moves to the next book in sequence – usually there is some choice, on which Mrs P decides.

Objectives
For each child to learn the skills of reading according to his stage of development.
For the children to learn to want to read and to enjoy books.

Strategy
Each child to read aloud to me every other day during activity periods (boys one day, girls the next).
To come to me for reading when I call them.
Evaluation through my tick book.
The 'Nippers' series to be introduced at some storytimes – the older children to be moved on to them when they finish their current books.
As the Animals topic develops children at all reading levels can move on to the Animals collection of books, as they finish their present book.
Other opportunities to read include work cards, flash cards, own writing, etc.

Resources
Set of 12 Nipper books.

Story

Context: Mrs P reads aloud for about fifteen minutes at the end of each day and chooses stories alternately more suitable for the older and then the younger children – but all are expected to listen.

Objectives

For the younger children to learn to listen and to enjoy stories.
For all, to link with other work and to extend their experience of spoken language.

Strategy

As far as possible uninterrupted reading; I shall attempt to dramatise my presentations and to make the stories 'larger than life'; each needs rehearsal the night before.
Evaluation of the stories impact – by impression from faces and subsequent discussion.

Resources

Older children's stories: Ursula Moray Williams *Adventures of the Little Wooden Horse* (nineteen chapters – one every other day).
Younger children's stories: Beatrix Potter's *Peter Rabbit Books*.

Topic

Context: During the six weeks I am following Mrs P's pattern of one major topic which lasts the whole time and three minor topics which are introduced as seems appropriate.

Major topic – Animals
Objectives

To provide stimulus for language development: spoken language, writing, and reading.
To provide resources for counting and sorting work of the younger children.
To provide ideas for creative art work – drawing, painting, claywork, possibly cardboard models.
To provide ideas for physical education.
To provide general knowledge about animals, and experience of 'finding out' in the context of the diagram opposite:

Strategies

Display of animal pictures to be put up on first day – change every few days some of the pictures, using items made by children or brought in by them.
Each day talk by me with class discussion (about ten minutes) about some aspect of animals – as a stimulus to work.
Each child to have an 'Animals' book for writing in.

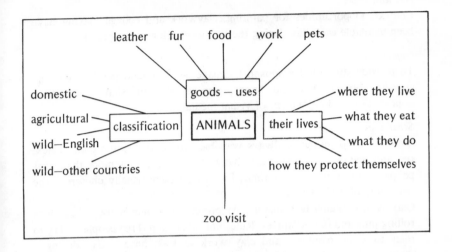

Reading books.
Visit to the local zoo.
(Possibly) classroom pets to be obtained, or borrowed.

Resources
Pictures of animals and other display items.
Set of writing books labelled with children's names and marked 'Animals'.

Reading books: four levels
yellow (pre-readers) – four home-made books consisting of animal pictures
  and the animals' names;
orange – ten books in Chambers' First Shelf series: *The Giraffe, The Tiger,
  The Camel, The Lion, The Monkey, The Elephant, The Polar Bear, The
  Husky Dog, The Arctic Fox, The Grey Seal*
red – eight books – *Ladybird Baby Animals* and *Big Animals*, Blackwell's
  British Animals 1 and *2*, and *Foreign Animals 1* and *2*, *The Junior True
  Book of Animal Babies, The Junior True Book of Animal Homes.*
brown – four books – Ginn's First Interest Series: *Starting Life, Save these
  Animals, Animal Defences, Animals keeping Clean.*
Books for me to read aloud:
  F.M. Branley's *Big Tracks, Little Tracks*
  T.S. Eliot's *Old Possum's Book of Practical Cats*
  B. Ireson's *Young Puffin Book of Verse* – section on animals
  Spike Milligan's *A Book of Milliganimals*

Minor topics (Details omitted – MB.)

Art and craft

Context: Opportunities for painting, claywork and collage making have been available each day during the half-term prior to my practice.

Objectives

To provide stimulus for spoken language development, possibly writing, coordination of eyes and hands, non-verbal expression, exploration, appreciation and enjoyment of visual media.

Strategies

Materials for painting are always available – three colours at present: black, red and yellow; at some stage change these. Rule: not more than four people painting at any one time; four to start are usually chosen at the beginning of each period.

Clay is also regularly available. At present only hands used. Introduce rolling pins and (blunt) knives. Rule: not more than three people ... Try to refer to some paintings and clay work at least once a day during a discussion time. Use children's work as a stimulus for other children's thinking. Regularly change wall display of art work done by children.

Collage. Materials available in trays. Set up a group of three or four at each period to work on the class ongoing collage. Subject: animals. Try to get the children to draw outlines, but give them some help.

Tie and dye. Introduce in about third week.

Box work. Introduce as replacement for collage in about fourth week.

Resources

Check paper and paints each morning.

Clay. Put out fresh pieces at beginning of each morning and afternoon. Put used clay, if not being kept, into 'wet' bucket at end of day.

Collage materials – check these each morning.

Play activities

Context: currently available activities – big bricks, little bricks, dressing up materials, home corner, dry sand, water trough, woodwork bench. Latter two to be removed before I start.

Objectives

To provide stimulus for spoken language development, cooperative social interaction, body co-ordination and exploration.

Strategies

Children choose activities, but numbers of children limited to: big bricks (3), little bricks (3), dressing up (3), home corner (4), dry sand (2).

Feature these activities from time to time in discussions. Comment on interesting ways in which children are working with them.

At some stage turn the home corner into a vet's surgery; introduce through discussion.

Change from dry sand to wet sand. Look out for children's ideas and follow them up. Animal plaques? Animal footprints? Possibly introduce plaster casts of hoofprints.

Get the bricks people to construct zoos sometimes.

Dressing up materials — new clothes require introduction.

Careful attention to tidying up is necessary!

Resources
Available in the classroom as cited above. New clothes needed.

Physical education
Context: The children have had regular lessons involving floorwork, small apparatus work and singing games, but have done no creative dance.

Objectives
To experience movement ideas through the rhythms of creative dance.
To extend vocabulary in terms of body, effort and space concepts.
To gain in self-confidence through the experience of movement.

Strategy
Outline plan for three lessons a week for six weeks:
Mondays — concentrating on Body Awareness:

stepping and running
leaping and striding
galloping and skipping
spinning and turning
hopping and jumping.

Wednesdays — concentrate on Effort:

speed: fast and slow
weight: heavy and light
speed: fast, medium and slow
weight: pushing and pulling
speed: gradual change from slow to fast (can they do this?)
weight: pressing and gripping.

Fridays — concentrate on Space:

near and far
above and below

forwards, backwards, sideways
straight and curved
turning and twisting
circling.

Each lesson to include:

warming up activities
development of one or two simple phrases, in relation to me
repeat of one or two of the phrases learned earlier
links with knowledge of animals where possible.

Each lesson to last for about twenty minutes, plus changing time.

Resources
Tambourine, gym slippers.

---

25   Daily forecast – stage four teaching:

(This is the imaginary forecast for one day of the practice outlined in briefs' 21 and 24 and relating to a class of infants who are vertically grouped.)

5.11.76 Forecast for Monday (Day six of practice)
Activity period one

9.30– 9.35   Instructions:
remind everybody about classroom procedures
starting activities: Susan and Anne must start writing now,
Keith must start numbers now, others may choose;
mention new painting colours – green and orange in place of
red and yellow;
gather group who are starting number bonds cards – John,
Peter, Mary ... (Details omitted – MB.)
'everybody else busy'.

9.35– 9.45   Explain to the number bonds group how they are to use the
work cards.

9.45–10.25   generally supervise
check on Susan, Anne, and Keith
check on number bonds group
hear eight boys read.

Activity period two

11.00–11.20   Dance in hall – 'leaping and striding' – body awareness.
1   Arrange for four little ones to be helped in changing.

2   Warming up. Shaking – each foot, leg, fingers, hands, arms, head, whole self.
3   Repeat 'stepping and running' phrases of last week.
4   Striding – 'stride and stride and stride and pause'.
5   Leaping – 'leap and pause, leap and pause, leap and pause'.
6   Tigers – roar.
7   Tiger striding – 'stride and stride and stride and listen'.
8   Tiger leaping – 'leap and watch, leap and watch, leap and catch your prey'

11.30–11.45   Class discussion – 'Tigers'

Strategy: Tiger – big, fierce, fast moving animal – lives in Asia – mountain woodland. Who has seen in zoo? Carnivorous. Colour scheme – camouflage. Babies – cubs. Try to involve Keith and Darryl. Introduce work cards.

Resources: pictures, work cards.

Activity period three
1.35– 1.40   Instructions
              'Who hasn't done any number work yet, writing?...' Stress tiger theme for writing.
              'Who would like to make a collage of a tiger?' (four children)
              'Everybody busy.'
1.40– 1.50   Help 'tiger' group – use pieces of yellow/brown carpet. Guide the outline shape only if necessary.
1.50– 2.25   Generally supervise.
              Hear ten boys read.

Last period
2.50– 3.25   Class discussion. Focus on some of the work done during the day.
              Story: chapter 3 of *The Little Wooden Horse*.

5.11.76 Evaluation
1   Number bonds work cards seem suitable except for some of yellow cards – rewrite.
2   PE went well. Tiger theme caught on. Pierre, Keith and Mary worked very well. Little ones a little lost. Peter a nuisance.
3   Tiger discussion rather flat. Needed bigger and better pictures.

4   Tiger collage started by Jane, Anne, Simon and Darryl. Needs more material.
5   Discussion time – Andrew offered to make collage of crocodile. Bring in egg boxes.

26   School notebooks – Stage four teaching: II

Brief 20 gave some suggestions for the kinds of notes and records which are appropriate for Stage four teaching – that is when you are working with most of the children for most of the time. Briefs 21–25 have given examples of such notes and records; this brief is an overview and commentary on these.

A chart of the notes and records helps to put them in perspective.

notes and records made before the practice	notes and records made each day of the practice	notes and records made afterwards
draw up overall forecast (Brief 21) draw up curriculum forecasts (or schemes of work) (Brief 24) start children's individual records (Brief 22)	during day keep daily record book (tick book) (Brief 23) after school write brief evaluation of the day (Brief 25) after school write forecast for tomorrow (Brief 25) after school write notes on a few individuals (Brief 22)	evaluate your forecasts evaluate your classroom performance evaluate yourself (Brief 47)

Four features of this approach are worth highlighting:

1   It should be possible to write the evaluation of 'today', the forecast for 'tomorrow' and a few individual notes on children, within one hour. This can be the case only if adequate preparation of curriculum forecasts has been done before the practice begins.
2   The forecast for 'tomorrow' concentrates on strategy with some reference to resources: objectives have been spelled out in the curriculum forecasts and in the individual records of the children.

CHART OF NOTES FOR A TEACHING PRACTICE

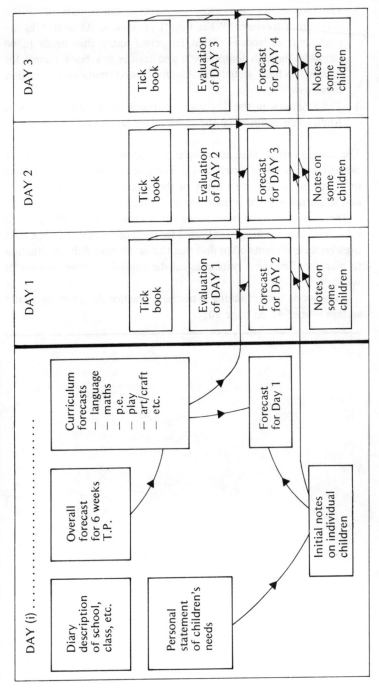

3   The forecast for 'tomorrow' is made in the context of (a) the curriculum forecasts (What have I planned to do next?) (b) the evaluation of 'today' (What happened today that needs to be followed through tomorrow?) and (c) the tick book record for 'today' (Which individual children need particular attention tomorrow?)
4   The emphasis in the forecast is as much on what the teacher is going to do as on what the children are going to do.

The daily forecasts here are simpler than those suggested earlier for Stages two and three (briefs 6–13). The assumption is that you have now learned to deal with many of the minor points of organization and so do not need to write these down regularly.

The examples have been based on a class of vertically grouped infant children working to pattern 4 for most of the day. This has been used because students often find that this is the most difficult situation to plan for. The same principles can be applied to other patterns of work.

Suggestions for evaluating a teaching practice are given in a later section – brief 47 on page 90.

SECTION TWO   CLASSROOM CONTROL

Most student-teachers have anxieties about classroom control and this topic merits regular discussion during the years of training. The difficulty for a tutor is to know what guidelines to offer his students, for not only is the ability of a student-teacher to exercise effective control a reflection of her personality and therefore a problematic area for discussion, but also there is little in the way of consensus among teachers as to what is meant by effective control.

The briefs of this section are concerned with practical ways in which a student-teacher can learn to assert herself and to get her own way with a class of children. Questions such as 'Ought the teacher to impose her will on the children?' are not considered, because the book is intended to be practical rather than philosophical. But discussion of these issues should be an essential part of a student's course and in this connection the book *Discipline in Schools*, edited by Turner (1973) (published by Ward Lock Educational) is recommended. The following quotation from Michael Duane's contribution to that book is pertinent:

Perhaps we may define the discipline of a school as being 'good' when teachers find that they enjoy and are stimulated by what they do; when the children are growing strong and vigorous; when they are learning fast and well what they themselves want to learn; when they are reaching new levels of sensitivity about themselves and others; when the parents see the school staff as colleagues; when they and other local people feel that the school is theirs in a very full sense of use and regard. Discipline is 'bad' when there is a cleavage between school and community; when teachers dislike or feel uninterested in their work; when pupils attend school only because they are forced to; when problems of discipline are always to the forefront of staffroom discussions; when the teachers' talk is peppered by the word and by examples of misdemeanours; when the teachers refer to the parents as people of an inferior culture or having lower standards than themselves; when they call parents into the school only in times of trouble.

Where discipline is good it is because both staff and children are deeply preoccupied and happy in their work and because the work has purpose for them. It does not mean that instances of indiscipline do not occur, but they are seen in perspective as something to be looked at and dealt with rationally. They do not distort the attitudes and the relations within the school.

The Plowden Report (1967) (Recommendation 94) contained a firm recommendation that 'the infliction of physical pain as a method of punishment in primary schools should be forbidden.' To date this has not been implemented; a recent survey of primary schools in Lancashire and Cumbria by Bennett (1976) (*Teaching Styles and Pupil Progress* p. 44) found that 'over half the teachers admitted to smacking.' Perhaps one of the reasons for the continuance of corporal punishment in schools is that teachers have had insufficient training in non-violent methods of maintaining control in their classrooms.

---

27 Children's expectations of their teacher

Much has been written about the consequences of teachers' expectations of their pupils, but curiously little has been said about pupils' expectations of their teachers. Yet failure to match up to pupils' expectations of teacher behaviour is the most likely reason why some student-teachers have discipline problems.

Nash (1976) ('Pupil expectations of their teachers' in Stubbs and Delamont (ed) *Explorations in classroom observation*, John Wiley) put it like this:

... children in British schools commonly expect their teacher to act as policeman and judge; a teacher who ignores this and behaves as if his task were simply to instruct or as if he will be accepted as a friend, counsellor and stimulator of ideas, is not likely to be perceived as he perceives himself. He will rather be categorized by pupils as 'soft' and incompetent, and be given little respect.

Nash carried out a series of structured conversations with individual members of a class of twelve year olds and elicited the following six characteristics as representing the children's view of appropriate behaviour by teachers.

1   Keeps order – is strict, punishes those who misbehave.
2   Teaches – keeps children busy so that they learn.
3   Explains – helps children who don't understand.
4   Is interesting – introduces variety and stimulates; isn't boring.

5   Is fair – is consistent, doesn't punish indiscriminately, has no favourites.
6   Is friendly. (This was seen as a bonus; the children didn't expect it, but were grateful when their teacher was friendly.)

Teacher and children do not act in the classroom in isolation from each other. The teacher's actions are partly determined by the children's actions and theirs by his. Also the teacher's actions are partly determined by his expectations of the children's actions and theirs by their expectations of his.

When children act in ways which the teacher thinks are inappropriate he is likely to see this as an infringement of the 'rules', even if this particular happening has hitherto not been specifically proscribed before. Similarly if the teacher acts in ways which the children think are inappropriate they will feel that he has broken their 'rules' and they may then act as though they have the right to misbehave.

---

28   Personal power of a teacher

If a student-teacher is to achieve educational objectives with her pupils, she needs to be able to exercise sufficient personal power to cause them to carry out the activities she has planned. Discussion of personal power, discipline and classroom control may seem distasteful, but if these are weak the student-teacher's planning is likely to be in vain.

It is worth stressing that the exercise of authority over thirty-five children is a very different matter to organizing two or three children at home. This is clear if one thinks of them all talking together, or all trying to go through one door at the same time.

Wadd (1972) ('Classroom Power', *Education for Teaching*, 89, 42–49) has suggested four factors which determine the personal power of a teacher over a class. These are:

1   his charisma
2   his mastery of subject matter
3   his ability to organize a class and
4   his ability to dominate a class when necessary.

It seems unlikely that an individual's charisma can be changed, but each of the others could conceivably be improved. Mastery of subject matter is of greater significance with older children, while the ability to organize is particularly important with young ones. Overall this book is about classroom organization in its many facets. What of dominance?

Dominance is a complicated art. Too little achieves little; too much

57

achieves the immediate result but intimidates people, probably to the detriment of their learning. One person achieves dominance over others by appropriate use of voice, by facial expression, by gesture, or by coming physically closer. Probably it is the deliberateness of speech and the intensity of eye contact that are the most powerful factors in achieving dominance.

Some students may find it helpful to practise projection of different levels of dominance in a room on their own. If possible, examine the impression that your physical presence and your gestures make by watching yourself in a mirror. For example, practice telling somebody to be quiet at different levels from 'Please stop talking!' (calm and quiet) to 'Stop talking this instant!' (loud and angry). Think of a number of difficult situations in school and practise your responses. Remember Pasteur's maxim, that chance favours the prepared mind!

---

29 Organization

'The devil makes work for idle hands, but keep 'em busy and you'll have no bother' is a sound piece of advice, ages old, and difficult for the inexperienced teacher to act on.

The art of keeping children busy can be broken down into two parts:

(i)   The children should know for every minute of the time that they are in the classroom, *what* it is that you want them to do, *where* and *when* they are to do it, and *what* they are to do *next*.

(ii) The children should *want* to do it.

The first point entails careful planning on your part of what, where, when and what next, and clear instructions which are reiterated as often as necessary. Some of these instructions will be minute by minute decisions uttered by you, others may be written down on work cards, while others will be the long-term rules of the classroom.

This does not mean that the classroom should be like a drill sergeant's parade ground. To tell every child exactly what he is to do for every minute of the day would be educationally disastrous. In a stimulating and well organized classroom, often that which the teacher wants the children to do (the 'what'), is to decide for themselves what they are going to do. But he has made it clear to them that *he wants* them to decide. In other words the teacher still controls the overall structure of the programme.

'What next' is an important element in giving instructions. With some classes there is a big difference between the instruction 'Go and line up by the door' and 'Go and line up by the door, waiting silently until I come.'

Particularly for young children it is wise to give 'follow through' instructions so that they are aware of what to expect next. Many student teachers miss the importance of this and get into difficulties in consequence.

The second point entails your careful choice of activity, adequate supervision, appropriate rewards for those who work in the way you expect, and disapprobation for those who don't.

Everybody has classroom failures. Try to analyse yours using the above points. After a teaching practice, if each member of a discussion group describes a problem of class control which she has experienced, a valuable exchange of ideas can occur.

---

30 Noise

In the past teachers did not permit children to chatter while working and the only noise in classrooms was that made by teachers. It is now widely recognized that chatter can contribute to the processes of learning, especially in terms of language development. Some teachers distinguish between 'busy noise' – which arises from children working, and 'lazy noise' or 'naughty noise' – which comes from children who are engaged in activities other than those prescribed by the teacher.

Why limit 'busy noise'? Four possible reasons are:

1 Excessive noise may prevent children from working, and some are more affected by a noisy environment than others. (However it is very unlikely that children need absolute quiet in order to concentrate their thinking.)

2 Excessive noise may affect the teacher so that he cannot function competently. This may be particularly so if he has a headache, etc.

3 Excessive noise may disturb other classes or groups of children who are trying to engage in quiet activities – such as listening to music. This can be a problem in open plan schools.

4 Student-teachers may be concerned about the impression given to headteacher or tutor if her children become too noisy.

Strategies for limiting noise can be 'negative' or 'positive'.

1 Examples of negative strategies:
'Turn the volume down, please.'
'You're getting too noisy. Will everyone try to be quieter.'
'Stop talking everybody! For the next ten minutes we will have absolute quiet.'

2 A positive strategy for limiting noise is one which focuses on the work

in hand rather than on the noise which it is generating. Example: (The class is becoming noisy. The teacher has been talking to one child.) 'May I interrupt everybody for one moment. Sharon has drawn an excellent graph which I would like you to look at.' (Holds it up.) 'I'd like you when your turn comes to try and do your graphs just as neatly. Alright. Carry on working.'

A similar strategy entails the teacher visiting a noisy group in the classroom and discussing their progress – rather than shouting at them across the room.

A final point. Noisy classes often have noisy teachers. Why?

---

31 Instructions

Giving instructions

From time to time most teachers find it necessary to interrupt the work of their classes in order to give instructions. Four steps can be recognized, although the extent to which each is necessary depends upon the training of the class.

(i)   Attract and hold everybody's attention.

       A quiet command like 'Everybody look this way, please' may be sufficient, the children recognizing your voice through the prevailing noise. If you have to shout try to lower your voice as soon as they have heard you. If necessary clap your hands or bang a book on the table.

       Once you have given a 'look this way' command, do not attend to individual children who ask a question. This is a common fault among the inexperienced; it quickly leads to the children starting again whatever they were doing when you interrupted them and means that you have to repeat your command.

       If some people have not stopped and turned towards you, increase your level of dominance and attract their attention by calling out their names and repeating the command.

       Aim to achieve eye to eye contact with every member of the class. This helps you to judge whether they understand what you say next.

(ii)   Give your instructions quickly and clearly.

       If the instruction entails movement by the children, make it clear at the beginning that they should not move until you say.

       Try to assess from their faces whether they have understood what it is they have to do. If you are in doubt ask one or two people.

If there is to be mass movement ensure that congestion is avoided.

(iii) Give the word to start.

(iv) Supervise events to ensure that your instructions are carried out.

Children's response to instructions
As a basis for discussion reflect on this:

The teacher gives an instruction (short or long term, positive or negative, to one child or to all, etc.) Each child either complies with or deviates from the behaviour which the teacher intended when she gave the instruction. Compliant or deviant behaviour may depend upon a number of factors:

(i) The nature of the instruction.

(ii) The understanding by the child of the instruction.

(iii) The remembering by the child of the instruction.

(iv) The interest of the child in carrying out the instruction.

(v) The awareness of the child of the teacher's supervision.

(vi) The effect on the child of the teacher's approval or disapproval.

(vii) The effect on the child of the other children's behaviour.

(viii) The previous training of the child in carrying out instructions.

Consider the following teachers' utterances in the light of these factors:
'As soon as you are all quiet you may go out to play.'
'During playtime you two boys will stay in the classroom and complete the writing which you should have done earlier.'
'Yesterday I said that nobody must drink their milk while sitting on the carpet.'
'Pick up your chair with two hands, carry it into the hall making sure that you don't bump anything with it, when you get there put your chair in line with the others, sit on it, fold your arms and don't talk.'

32 Punishment

Most teachers regard punishing children as a regrettable but necessary part of the process of helping children to become social beings. Punishment is used to stop children behaving in ways that teachers consider to be undesirable, to train children so that they share teachers' values about what is undesirable behaviour, and to enable them to act on their own initiative according to those values. We punish children in order that punishment may become unnecessary. In practice, punishment frequently fails to produce the results we want and often has consequences we do not want.

One approach to discussion of punishment is to identify three components: power assertion, justification and affective withdrawal. When the offending event occurs, or is revealed, the teacher asserts his power by dominating the situation and giving a punishment. At the same time, explicitly or implicitly, he justifies his action. For a period following the punishment, he keeps affectively distant from the offender.

Power assertion can be manifest in terms of five main forms of punishment which are used by teachers in Britain:

1 By giving a verbal reproof – either in public or more-or-less in private. (This may be linked to one of the following.)
2 By depriving the child of a pleasurable activity, e.g. 'stay in at playtime'.
3 By giving the child an unpleasant activity to do, e.g. 'sit with your hands on your head'.
4 By inflicting pain; (this is not permissible for student-teachers and the argument that 'violence breeds violence' suggests that it should not be used by any teacher).
5 By referring the child to a more powerful authority, e.g. headteacher or parent.

Justification of punishment is of three kinds:
1 The teacher focuses on the child and the event and says how wrong, wicked, naughty, etc. the child has been.
2 The teacher focuses on himself in relation to the child and says how displeased he is with the child's behaviour.
3 The teacher focuses on the action and tries to make the child understand why it was undesirable.

Affective withdrawal is a way of expressing the diminution of personal relationship between the teacher and child that inevitably follows punishment. Thus the teacher is less likely to smile at the child, tends to ignore him or talks to him more sharply than usual.

Points for discussion:

What examples of the five forms of punishment have you seen?
What kinds of punishment would you reckon to use?
What are the likely consequences of each of the three kinds of justification listed above?
After affective withdrawal, what can a teacher do to re-establish personal relationships with a child?
What is the likely consequence of setting extra work as a punishment?

(This analysis is based on Derek Wright's contribution to *Discipline in Schools*, edited by Turner (1973) published by Ward Lock Educational, pp. 33–44. In places he is quoted verbatim.)

33   What to try with a disruptive child

Most classes have some children who are difficult from time to time; a few have the child who totally disrupts the work of the rest of the class frequently. What do you do with him? Your personality, temperament, experience, and liking for the child will all play a part in helping him to conform to the norms of behaviour of the classroom. It may be appropriate, however, to treat him exceptionally. This brief contains some suggestions for a systematic approach to modify his behaviour.

These suggestions depend upon your being able to find some simple rewards and punishments which become significant to the child and then applying them rigorously over several weeks.

1   Make a list of the undesirable behaviours in which the child engages, and then decide on three major ones which you will try to extinguish during the next few weeks. Write these undesired behaviours and their converse on a chart. Decide on some simple rewards and punishments and put these on the chart as well, with columns so that you can enter the number of times you give them on each day of the week. See p. 64. Also prepare some cards, one for each day, which the child can keep and on which he can stick stars for good behaviour.

2   Talk to the child on his own and tell him that you are going to help him to be like the other people in the class. Encourage him to say that he will help you to help him. Show him your chart and explain what things you want him to do and what you don't want him to do. Tell him how you will punish undesirable behaviour. Give him his chart for the day and tell him that for every quarter of an hour for which he is well-behaved, you will give him a star to stick on his card. If he gets four stars in a day you will let him do a job for the class. If he gets eight stars you will ask the head if he may ring the school bell at the end of afternoon school. Show him where to hang the card on the wall. Tell him that you are going to ask all the rest of the class to help him.

3   Briefly and simply tell the whole class that the child is trying to behave like everybody else and ask them to help him. Tell them about the star chart and his possible rewards. Don't labour the points and don't hector the child.

4 This is an example of a teacher's chart for a particular child:

DESIRED BEHAVIOUR not molesting other children staying in his place not shouting out in lessons						UNDESIRED BEHAVIOUR molesting other children wandering around the classroom shouting out in lessons					
Mon	Tue	Wed	Thu	Fri	Rewards	Punishments	Mon	Tue	Wed	Thu	Fri
					star on personal chart	stand facing wall for 3 mins					
					monitor jobs or teacher's errands	stay in during playtime					
					ring school bell at end of day	send to headteacher					

5 The child's card is much simpler. It doesn't say what it is used for, but just has his name and the day and date. A punched hole enables it to be hung on a nail on the wall.

PETER	Monday 13 December

6 Reward the child frequently at first. As suggested above, one quarter of an hour may be the right interval to start with. It may be advantageous to use a kitchen pinger to remind you when the fifteen minutes is up and also to remind you when his three minutes of punishment is up; it adds to the children's sense of fairness if the time intervals are rigorously kept. After a few days, increase the time interval to twenty minutes, perhaps change the colour of the stars; tell him that he is improving and that you are pleased. Later move to half an hour and then to longer periods. Try to concentrate on the three behaviours that

you have selected as important – if he mutters to himself or picks his nose, forget it. Keep the record carefully so that you can monitor progress. If it works, when you take him off the star cards, make a class event of it and give him some regular job as his reward.

Agreed – it's horrible trying to manipulate somebody else's behaviour! But sometimes for the sake of the child, for your sanity and that of the class, you have to take exceptional measures. If it seems too much trouble to go through this procedure, you haven't got a disruptive child but just a normal mischief-maker!

Obviously you should try to discover the origin of the child's undesirable behaviour because this is likely to be the best way of helping him. But don't be fobbed off with the simplistic answer of 'trouble at home'. Lots of children have trouble at home and only a few disrupt the classroom in consequence. Ask yourself if the disruptive behaviour is triggered off by your handling of the situation. (Based on an article by Tom Crabtree in *Teacher's World*, 9 April 1976.)

---

34   What to try if a riot breaks out

It may never happen, but if it does it will be as well to have thought out an effective strategy beforehand!

The essential ideas behind the following sequence of possible events are:

(i)   Don't lose your self-control. Keep your dignity and help the children to try to keep theirs. Remember that afterwards you all have to live together. In particular, do not hit anybody; apart from the moral aspect of the legitimacy of violence, you are not allowed as a student-teacher to give physical punishment.

(ii)   Remember that they expect you to regain control and all the moderates will want you to.

(iii)   Project your personality dramatically. Vary the volume and emphasis of your voice, use pauses; make dominant gestures such as hands on hips, or arms folded, or point.

(iv)   Don't drag out the reprimand once you have re-established calm; move quickly into purposeful activity that keeps everybody busy.

Some suggestions in sequence

1   Perhaps you arrive in the classroom to find many people shouting, pushing and fighting, or during your lesson you suddenly realize that matters have got out of hand. In a loud voice say something like 'Class 3. Stop what you are doing and look this way.' (This can be preceded by

a loud noise made by banging a book on a table or by clapping your hands – but beware the feeble clap which the children repeat!)

2   Two likely responses:
   (a)   Everybody stops and looks at you. *Quickly* and in a *quiet*, firm and perhaps angry voice make it quite clear that rowdy behaviour is not acceptable. Don't labour it; once you have made the point change tack and start work immediately on something that requires their individual attention. If the trouble started because the previous work misfired, it may be as well to tackle something different.
   (b)   Some people stop but others continue being rowdy. If you have a louder voice, use it to repeat your command for silence. Possibly move nearer to the offenders and glower. If it isn't working try the movement ploy. 'Everybody stand up, keep quiet and look at me.' Or, if they are standing, sit down. An extreme form of the movement ploy is to tell them to stand on their chairs, or to move out of the classroom and line up outside. The idea of movement is that the moderates will quickly obey you, those who didn't hear the instruction will realize what you have said, and anyone who chooses to continue to misbehave becomes more isolated and thus more noticeable. Move close and dominate by voice and gesture. 'Peter Brown and John Robinson' (very loud – then change to a loud and fierce whisper) 'I told you to stand up and be quiet.' The whisper gives the impression that there is another authority around.
         If it works proceed as in (a). If not, turn to 3.

3   If you are still in difficulty try one, or all, of these:
   (a)   Repeat the earlier sequence.
   (b)   Fold your arms, say nothing, and wait – while watching everybody like a hawk. (But if there is the likelihood of damage to children or property you must interfere.) Writing the names of miscreants on the chalkboard may help.
   (c)   Recognize that the situation is beyond your control and send one of the moderates for a teacher or the head.

4   Afterwards, ask yourself whether it was your fault that it happened. Could you have seen some early warning signs and taken more prompt action?

'Story time'

This is a simulation exercise for a group of about a dozen students working with a tutor. One student takes the role of 'teacher' while the others sit on the floor, or on chairs, in front of her. The 'teacher' reads a story to the 'class'. The tutor stands behind the 'teacher', out of her vision, and from time to time signals to members of the class to engage in deviant behaviour according to a finger code. For example, if he points at one student and then holds up four fingers, she is to molest her neighbour. As soon as the 'teacher' notices the deviant behaviour she is to act in any way she feels to be effective. The group then discuss her action. For example:

Jane, the 'teacher', is reading aloud to the group. The tutor points to Mary and holds up four fingers. Suddenly Mary digs John in the ribs.

Jane: Mary! Why did you do that?
Tutor: Fine, hold it a minute. Now, Jane, you did three things as soon as you spotted what Mary did. First, you frowned at her; then you said 'Mary!' in a sharp voice and then 'Why did you do that?' Have you any comments to make?
Jane: Perhaps I should have stopped after I said 'Mary!' My question would have led to a disciplinary discussion which would have interrupted the story.
Mary: Actually, I reckon the look you gave me, Jane, was sufficient to stop most of the kids I meet.
John: If just a frown was sufficient to make Mary stop misbehaving, it would avoid disrupting the story for everybody else.
Tutor: Yes. OK. Let's continue. Carry on reading, 'teacher'.

Instructions for this exercise are given in the following brief.

---

35   Classroom control simulation 1: 'Story time'

Teacher's instructions
   (i)   You are going to read a story to the class. Of late they have been somewhat unruly and you have decided to be firm and stop any restless or disruptive behaviour.
   (ii) The class is sitting in front of you.
   (iii) Read the story and look up from time to time in order to check any difficult behaviour.
   (iv) When the tutor indicates, end the story and line up the class by the door.
   NB   During this exercise the tutor will be standing behind you, out of your vision and signalling to members of the class!

Class instructions
  (i)   Sit in front of the 'teacher' listen to the story and carry out any instructions given by the 'teacher', except –
  (ii) If the tutor points at you and holds up a number of fingers, carry out the activity suggested in the finger code.

Finger code
  (i)   Fidget.
  (ii)   Ask if you can go to the toilet.
  (iii) Whisper to a neighbour.
  (iv)   Molest a neighbour.
  (v)   Mutter 'Sister Eileen saw a diesel engine' (This can be done without moving the lips.)
  Open palm: stop.

'Matchsticks'

This is a simulation exercise which lasts for about eight minutes. It is not interrupted by the tutor as in 'Story time' but is analysed afterwards by the group. An audio cassette recording can be helpful in the follow up discussion, or, better, a video recording. Some students find this kind of role play with their peers quite difficult, but the effort required to carry it off can be very valuable for people who find problems in projecting their personality.

---

36   Classroom control simulation 2: 'Matchsticks'

Teacher's instructions
  (i)   You are going to instruct the 'class' on the making of matchstick towers.
  (ii)   The class sit at tables in front of you. A pile of matchboxes is on a nearby table.
  (iii) Throughout the exercise check any undesirable behaviour and correct anyone who does not carry out your instructions precisely.
  (iv)   Express the following points in your own words to give as clear instructions as possible.
    (a) 'Collect a matchbox and take it to your own work place.'
    (b) 'Build a tower using parallel pairs of matchsticks. Ensure that all the match heads point in the same direction.'
    (c) 'When you have finished, do not call out but put your hand up.'
    (d) 'Work quickly and don't talk to each other.'

(v)   When people have finished their tower, check that it is properly
       made. If it is wrong insist on it being rebuilt. If all is correct ask
       people to try to make a triangular tower.
(vi) After about six minutes tell everybody:
       (a) 'Stop work and look at me.'
       (b) 'Put the matches back in the box.'
       (c) 'Put the matchboxes back on the side table.'
       (d) 'Sit quietly with arms folded.'

Class instructions

Student 1   Start to carry out each instruction as soon as the teacher has
            uttered it.
Student 2   Lay your matches with the heads pointing at random.
Student 3   Lay 4 matches and then idle until the teacher admonishes you.
            Lay 4 more and idle again; but pretend to be busy!
Student 4   Discuss the temperature of the room with your neighbour.
Student 5   When your tower is half built ask your neighbour to lend you 2
            matches. If he/she refuses, pull his/her hair.
Student 6   When your tower is complete don't put your hand up – as
            instructed, but call out 'I've finished.'
Student 7   At a suitable point, go to sleep.
Student 8   When the teacher tells you to put the matches back in the box,
            light one ... when admonished say it was an accident.

'Getting cross'
This is the most difficult of these exercises; it requires the 'teacher' to act
anger. It is an opportunity of practising dominance in a controlled setting.
   Obviously these simulations cannot be a substitute for first-hand
experience of handling trouble-makers in the classroom, but they can be a
useful adjunct by helping students to recognize some of the skills which
they need to acquire and also in providing limited opportunities for
developing these skills.

---

37   Classroom control simulation 3: 'getting cross'

Teacher's instructions
In your view the class has been 'silly' most of the day and several times you
have had to reprimand individuals. It is necessary to move some chairs
from one side of the room to the other. Organize the class to carry the chairs
and to put them in a straight line.
If people misbehave be as cross as seems appropriate.

Class instructions

Student 1 Sorry – you are chosen for the teacher's wrath. When carrying your chair swing it above your head and, 'accidentally' (and gently) hit someone with it.

Student 2 During the ticking off whisper to your neighbour and then giggle. Repeat until you are reprimanded.

Student 3 During the ticking off ask if you can go to the toilet.

Other students: try to cooperate with the teacher.

SECTION THREE   CLASSROOM SKILLS

This section focuses attention on some of the basic skills which teachers use day by day.

38   Printing and handwriting

All primary school teachers need to be able to write neatly and legibly with various media and in different sizes of lettering. Carry out the following lettering exercises and display them on a convenient wall with the work of the other students in your group. Put your name and the time on each sheet.

(i)   On an A4 sheet of plain paper copy the letter shapes of the diagram on p. 72, aiming to make each tall letter 2cm high and using biro, fountain pen or pencil.

(ii)   Repeat using a thick felt pen. (Which is easier?)

(iii)   On an A4 sheet of plain paper, write the following in your neatest handwriting. (No guidelines allowed!) Pay careful attention to spacing.

> You may give them your love, but not your thoughts,
> For they have their own thoughts.
> You may house their bodies, but not their souls,
> For their souls dwell in the house of tomorrow, which you cannot visit, not even in your dreams.
> You may strive to be like them, but seek not to make them like you,
> For life goes not backward nor tarries with yesterday.
>
> Kahil Gibran

Does your writing need to improve? Are you too slow at neat lettering? Can you work neatly without guidelines? Do you need practice?

If your handwriting is illegible to other people, do something about it. Acquire a legible style such as Marion Richardson's cursive writing or the italic writing of John Le Dumpleton's *Handwriting* (Teach Yourself Books, EUP, 1955).

When you first visit a school for school practice, find out if a particular style of letters is used. For example, do the teachers put a curly tail on the letter 't'? This is particularly important to some infant teachers. Similar practice of the above exercises on a chalkboard is worthwhile.

71

Aa Bb Cc Dd Ee Ff Gg Hh Ii Jj Kk Ll Mm Nn Oo Pp Qq Rr Ss Tt Uu Vv Ww Xx Yy Zz

39 Work cards

A work card is a means of structuring a child's learning experience with the minimum of attention from the teacher. It enables the teacher to concentrate his attention on particular children while the others are working from cards.

Work cards, if properly designed, allow children to work at their own level while encouraging independence and responsibility for their own work.

A further value to the beginning reader is that work cards usually provide reading experience.

However, work cards require careful construction in order to be effective instruments of individual learning. Like all forms of teaching they should be appropriate to the nature of the activity and to the abilities and interests of the individual child; the teacher therefore needs to be familiar with both. (This material is based on a handout by S. P. Leigh.)

Types of work card

A *Partial instructions* These need oral explanation by the teacher or by an experienced child. Simple tasks for young infants can be set up in this way, for example matching, counting, sorting, copying, colour recognition. The teacher or another child explains what needs to be done and the child then works through a set of cards. Pictures, numbers, symbols and/or words are used to convey meaning.

B *Full instructions* These are cards needing no further explanation and are usually appropriate for older infants and juniors. They may initiate various kinds of work:

   1 Guiding observations from first hand experience – visits, experiments, etc.
   2 Finding information in reference materials and communicating it in various ways – writing, drawing, map-making, calculating, modelling, etc.
   3 Giving instructions for practical work and recording – science, mathematics, craftwork, etc.

Content

1 The wording needs to be such that the vocabulary and conceptual level is appropriate for the child. Particular words may need class discussion and/or display as labels on apparatus or as a picture dictionary.

2 The teacher should be clear on her objectives in writing a card. Compare:

Example A   How many legs has a bee? Where do bees live? What food do bees make for us? How does a bee attack its enemies?

Example B   Find out about bees. Write an article for a children's magazine starting: 'Yesterday I was stung by a bee. Do you know about bees? Let me tell you about them ...'

3   When the instruction is to obtain information from reference books (i.e. with juniors) it is worth suggesting ways of interpreting or expressing the information in order to avoid mere copying or paraphrasing. For example:

    Writing in the first-person as though involved or as an eye witness.
    Writing as though for a newspaper or TV report.
    Expressing personal reactions to the information.
    Presenting the information in a different form − oral (tape recorder?), graphic, symbolic, dramatic, etc.

4   Sometimes it may be useful to initiate group work through a work card with each member of the group taking a share in the tasks.

5   In a series of cards progression to more advanced tasks is necessary so that children do not remain at one level for too long. The teacher needs to constantly review progress − more able children may omit some cards in a series, while slower learners may need extra cards.

Layout

1   Card is better than paper because it is more durable. If it is to be used for some time covering with transparent film ('Contact' or 'Fablon') or brushing with paper varnish ('Isobond') may be worthwhile.

2   The size should be convenient for handling and storing.

3   The writing needs to be appropriate for the reader − large printing and few words for infants, small printing for young juniors, joined script or typing for older juniors.

4   Coding is usually helpful to teacher and children − colour of card, coloured stars, numbers, symbols etc.

5   If materials or reference books are required it is worth making this clear − possibly on the reverse side.

74

Display and storage

1 A set of hanging pockets made from heavy cloth may be useful for displaying the cards and making for ready access; this can be pinned to the classroom wall or the end of a cupboard.

2 A storage box with dividers may be useful for when the cards are not in use. Storage is easier if all the cards are the same size.

References
Useful points about work cards are made in:

TAYLOR, J. (1971) *Organising and Integrating the Infant Day* Unwin Chapter 3 (Infants)

HASLAM, K. R. (1971) *Learning in the Primary School* Unwin Chapter 5 (Juniors)

---

40 Classroom display

Primary school classrooms usually have delightful displays on the walls, side tables, and sometimes hanging from the ceiling. Why? Here is a list of some of the objectives which teachers may have in mind when putting up displays.

1 To provide an initial stimulus to learning through a display which sparks off discussion, enquiry or creative work – e.g. a display of yellow things, some broken clocks or paper snowflakes.

2 To record the recent work of the class – e.g. a map of 'where we live' might be a record of investigations about the neighbourhood, or a collage of a fireman might commemorate a visit by the fire-brigade.

3 To reinforce recent learning – e.g. the collage of a fireman might be used in class discussions with flash cards to reinforce the recognition of certain words.

4 To provide information needed for individual work – e.g. a number chart, a picture dictionary, a poster with information.

5 To give motivation to children to work by the promise of display – e.g. 'Make a collage of a lion and we will display it on the wall.' 'If you do your very best writing I will put it up on the wall.'

6 To promote aesthetic sensitivity to colour, shape, texture, composition, etc. – e.g. through the choice of display and through the mounting, framing, backing, labelling, etc.

7 To provide an attractive and cheerful environment which heartens children, teachers, parents and visitors.

If you have been responsible for putting up displays on a classroom wall it is a worthwhile exercise afterwards to make a rough sketch of the wall, with the various items, and to write against each item the key numbers which relate it to the above list of objectives. In other words this exercise requires you to justify your display. The following questions may stimulate further thoughts.

(a) Taking each displayed item in turn, what do the children gain from it?
(b) How long should each item stay on the wall?
(c) Has the time taken to put up the display been commensurate with what it achieves?
(d) Could the display space be used more effectively?
(e) Have you displayed those items which need to be read, or examined closely, so that the children can reach them?

---

41   Classroom A/V aids

Some people have little difficulty working with classroom aids such as projectors and tape recorders; others waste valuable teaching-time trying to get the equipment to work.

Reading about how to operate a machine is usually a poor way of learning; there is no substitute for working with the actual machine. What is appropriate here is to give a check list of equipment which may be available in a primary school and to suggest that you find opportunities to practise using each.

record player (including how to change the needle)
audio tape recorder
audio cassette recorder (including how to make good classroom recordings)
slide projector (including how to change the bulb)
filmstrip projector
8 mm film projector
16 mm film projector
overhead projector
camera
spirit duplicator
ink duplicator
heat copier or photocopier.

One skill that is worth describing is that of making clear audio recordings of your own speech in the classroom. The secret of success is to carry a cassette recorder and wear the microphone about 10 to 15 cm below your mouth. If the recorder hangs at your waist from a strap either over one shoulder, or worn diagonally across the chest, with the microphone fixed by rubber bands to the carrying strap at the top of your chest, very good recordings of what you say can be made, and usually it is possible to tell what children have said to you. This is much more satisfactory than trying to fix up a microphone from the ceiling, or positioning it on a desk.

This procedure enables one to make recordings irrespective of whether standing in one place, sitting down, or walking round the classroom. Listening to recordings of oneself in action in the classroom should be a regular part of learning to teach. Many different ways of analysing one's talk are available, from listening for repetitious mannerisms to identifying the kinds of talk which children make in response to one's own speech. Joan Tough's work is relevant to the latter. (*Listening to Children Talking*, Ward Lock Educational, 1976.)

---

42 Telling and reading stories

Telling stories is probably more appropriate for younger children. It is a more intimate, personal experience and material can be adapted in the telling to meet the needs of the class and the situation.
Reading stories is usually better for older children. (These ideas are based on a handout by S. P. Leigh.)

Selection of stories
  (i) Stories need to be suitable for the particular children in terms of interest, vocabulary, ideas, characterization, action and humour.
 (ii) They should have a quality of directness, especially if to be told, i.e. not too complex, subtle or reflective.
(iii) The teacher must have sufficient sympathy with the story to be able to enter unreservedly into the telling or reading.
(iv) The quality and size of illustrations may be a consideration with younger children.

Adaptation is sometimes necessary, e.g. shortening, omitting, condensing, modernising, or simplifying, according to the needs of the particular class.
Sometimes the whole story may be read (or told) at a time; sometimes part of it. With a long story it may be sufficient to read part and arouse enough interest for individual children to finish it for themselves.

Time and place

Normally about ten to fifteen minutes for younger children and up to thirty minutes for older children is appropriate.

If the children can gather close to the reader in a corner of the room this helps to create a feeling of intimacy in a shared experience.

Performance

A good performance comes essentially from the involvement of the teacher in the material, and the attempt to bring it alive by projection. Stories need to be dramatised and presented larger than life.

A good vocal technique is the result of a serious attempt to convey meaning, atmosphere and character. This can be aided by attention to:

(i)   *Audibility* This may be a question of speed of delivery – slower, more deliberate than conversational speech; volume – so that all can hear; and articulation – more pronounced than in conversation.

(ii) *Variety* Meaning is conveyed by changes in speed, emphasis, volume, and pitch.
      These changes should only be made in the service of the story, and not for their own sake. The aim is better communication, not better voice-production.

(iii) *Pauses* Use of a pause is necessary to separate sections, sentences and phrases so that meaning can be made clearer, and to stress a climax.

Looking up at the children from time to time assists in the sharing of the experience. The next few words are memorized, and a finger kept on the line while the teacher glances around at the children. This also enables the children's reactions to be assessed.

Gestures may be used for emphasis at certain points, but should be sparing.

With younger children the illustrations can enrich the experience. At appropriate moments they can be shown to the children, but without prolonged comment so as not to impede the flow of the story.

Questioning can interrupt imaginative concentration and is perhaps best left to the end or omitted. Any vocabulary difficulties can be met by explaining in parenthesis, or adding other words of similar meaning.

Stories can be followed by discussion with at least three different purposes:

(i)   To deepen the experience. 'Which part did you like best?' 'Why did he do that?' 'What sort of person was he?' 'Have you ever felt like that?' 'Shall I read that bit again?'

(ii) To provide opportunity for purposeful speech by individual children.

(iii) To provide stimulus for futher activities, e.g. creative writing, dramatisation, art and craft, finding further information. A story can be the starting point for a project or topic, if sufficient interest is aroused.

Where possible the book should be displayed in the classroom, to allow children to read it for themselves.

The importance of practice

Unless you are experienced at reading aloud it is very worthwhile to start practising regularly. Aim to read aloud for at least ten minutes every day. This could be from newspaper or textbook, but reading from a chiildren's storybook is better because of the opportunities for impersonating different voices and dramatisation. Find a room on your own – maybe a bathroom – and never mind if your family or flat-mates laugh at you!

When you have gained sufficient self-confidence ask a fellow student, friend or tutor to listen to you read and to comment in these terms:

(i)   *Fluency* Does the reading flow or jerk? If it is jerky is it because the reader is failing to read ahead of her speech? Does she stumble over words which should have been practised beforehand?

(ii) *Articulation* Are the words clear and deliberate? Is emphasis being put in the right places?

(iii) *Delivery* Is it too fast or too slow? Are there appropriate pauses?

(iv) *Variation* Does the reader alter her pitch, pace, volume and emphasis sufficiently to dramatise the reading?

If you have difficulties with spoken English you may find the exercises given in Christabel Burniston's *Speech in Practice* (1955) helpful.

---

43   Classroom discussions

Language development is an essential concern of primary schools. Beyond the skills of oracy and literacy it has basic implications for much cognitive growth and, through that, for the ability to benefit from education generally. For these reasons classroom discussions are an important feature of the work of primary schools. This brief is concerned with classroom discussions which are led by the teacher. It is based on a handout by S. P. Leigh, and influenced by the work of Joan Tough.

There are two main elements in this kind of classroom discussion:

(a) the acts of talking and reading aloud by the teacher in which children receive information, instructions, ideas and feelings; and
(b) the acts of questioning by the teacher which are designed to elicit responses from the children.

If the teacher pays due regard to the conceptual, grammatical and lexical content of his talk and reading, the children meet models of language usage which they may later use themselves. If he also pays attention to the kinds of question he asks, he can directly elicit different kinds of language usage. This latter point is illustrated by the following table which relates types of question to types of language which may be elicited.

PROCESS	TYPE OF QUESTION	LANGUAGE USAGE
Description	What ...? Who ...? When ...? Where ...?	labelling things, people, (nouns); actions (verbs); qualities (adjectives, adverbs); relations (prepositions, conjunctions)
Classification	What is the same ...? What is different ...?	sorting items into classes; finding common properties and class names
Seriation	Which is first, last, bigger, biggest ...?	ordering items in terms of properties; language of comparison
Explanation	Why ...? How ...?	deducing and inferring relationships; language of rationality
Speculating	What would happen if ...? What could happen if ...?	inferring future events; use of conditional statements
Evaluation	What do you think of ...? What do you feel about ...?	making judgments; expressing feelings

Imagination	Suppose that ... Invent a ...	creating imaginary things and events; using similes and metaphors
Problem solving	Can you find out ...?	language of structured discovery
Question asking	What can you ask ...?	language of unstructured discovery

This list is not a comprehensive analysis of all possible questions, but a simple checklist which a student-teacher can use to help her reflect on her classroom questioning.

Make a tape recording of yourself leading a classroom discussion and afterwards play it back and analyse your questions into the above nine categories. A common finding is that most of the questions are of description and seriation, with the other categories rather neglected. If this is the case it is worth carrying out the following exercise. When you are waiting somewhere on your own, say in a bus queue, fix on some object, say a tree, and think up a series of questions which embrace all nine categories. Practise this regularly and your classroom questioning will become much more valuable.

Remember that language interaction is influenced by its context. There is the context of relationships; if relationships are warm and friendly there is likely to be better language response than if the reverse applies. The social context also affects language interaction; different children respond differently according to whether they are in an individual, small-group or large-group situation. The task context is also significant: some children are better at listening than talking, or at asking questions than at answering them.

There are many skills involved in leading a discussion. The teacher needs to stimulate and encourage involvement of everybody if possible. He needs to guide the focus of attention. If somebody's contribution is not clear he aids the discussion by clarifying the point made. He needs to balance the contributions by restricting the prominent speakers and encouraging the quieter people. As well as leading he should sometimes participate in the discussion by offering his own experience or ideas. And he should be quiet as frequently as possible in order to listen. But above all he needs to keep the discussion 'open' so that language is kept flowing and not brought to an abrupt halt. He needs to ask questions which open the discussion rather than ones which close it.

Thus the question 'Can you tell us about it?' is more likely to keep the discussion going than 'What is it?' likewise 'What does it make you feel?' is more useful than 'Do you like it?' Questions which lead to a variety of answers rather than to one clear cut response are valuable. Sometimes asking children to comment on each other's contributions helps to keep the discussion open.

Effective leadership of classroom discussions is not easy, but the skills can be learned through practice and reflection.

44 Marking and motivating in the classroom

Consider the following motivating strategies which a teacher may use to encourage his pupils to produce their best work.

1 Teacher marks child's work:
  (a) in his presence, and
      (i)   gives oral encouragement or reproof
      (ii)   holds discussion about child's difficulties
      (iii) gives instructions as to next work to be tackled.
  (b) in his absence, and
      (i)   gives written encouragement or reproof
      (ii)   gives written instructions as to next work to be tackled
      (iii) subsequently sees child to discuss difficulties.

2 Teacher gives child public encouragement:
  (a) by oral praise in front of class
  (b) by awarding a star or house point etc.
  (c) by displaying child's work on the wall
  (d) by permitting child to take work home to show parents
  (e) by sending child to head teacher to show work.

What are the advantages and disadvantages of these? By what criteria can they be judged? What is the effect of the teacher's method of marking on each child's work: does he act on the teacher's advice; do the teacher's rewards actually encourage him – or in practice do they have the reverse effect? How far does the effort put in by the teacher in his marking have a pay-off in terms of the children's work? If the teacher marks too little work, what happens? How does the teacher ensure that particular points he makes in his marking are acted on?

Consider the effect on a child of the following comments written by the teacher in his book:

Tick and teacher's initials.
'Good work'; 'This is not your best'; 'Poor writing'.

'I like the story but your writing is very untidy.'
'The story would have been more interesting if you had described what happened next.'
'It is time you tackled the work cards on PUNCTUATION.'

As with every other aspect of teaching there are objectives which can be identified as the purposes of marking, and strategies can be devised to contribute to their achievement.

---

45 Curriculum organization – objectives, strategies and problems

It is not the purpose of this book to examine the content of the curriculum of primary schools, but it is appropriate to look at some of the processes involved in the various curriculum activities and subjects. It is hazardous to divide the primary school curriculum into parts because many teachers aim to keep it integrated – and there are many different ways of sub-dividing it for those who choose to. But in order to focus on what takes place in the classroom it is necessary to effect some division, as has been done here.

This brief examines several of the major areas of the curriculum in terms of typical overall objectives which teachers may have, of typical learning strategies, and of some of the organizational problems. The main purpose of the brief is to remind the reader of the many curriculum skills which she needs to master in order to be an effective teacher of young children. The lists are inevitably incomplete and, alas inevitably, will be found to contain some learning strategies which some teachers would eschew.

Language
Objectives
1   To develop language skills: thinking, talking, listening, reading aloud, reading silently, writing, spelling, handwriting ...
2   To acquire a rich vocabulary and to use it appropriately according to context.
3   To experience pleasure in using language.

Learning strategies: spoken language
1   Discussion led by teacher with (a) class, (b) group, and (c) individuals.
2   Informal classroom discussion between children and between children and teacher in relation to various curriculum activities.
3   Group discussion structured by teacher who supervises, but is present for only part of the time.
4   Teacher reads aloud – stories, poems, etc.

Learning strategies: reading

1 Children respond to prereaders by discussing pictures, etc.
2 Teacher initiates reading skills by:
    (a) look and say (word recognition)
    (b) phonic 1 (letter sounds, digraphs and diphthongs)
    (c) phonic 2 (based on syllables)
    (d) sentence method.
3 Teacher and children use traditional orthography *or* the initial teaching alphabet.
4 Children read
    (a) silently
    (b) silently while listening to a tape recording of the text through headphones
    (c) aloud to the teacher
    (d) aloud to other adults.
5 Children read
    (a) their own writings
    (b) the teacher's writings – class-made books, work cards, flash cards, picture dictionaries, labels, etc.
    (c) reading books: the children progress through a sequential reading scheme, devised by teacher or school, to their own choice of books from the library
    (d) reference books and text books.

Learning strategies: writing

1 Children begin to write by drawing a picture, teacher writes description as given by child, child first traces on top of teacher's writing, later copies teacher's writing underneath; child reads his writing back to teacher.
2 Teacher stimulates writing through discussion, pictures, displays, filmstrips, films, TV, visitors, visits, etc.
3 Children obtain words for their writing from:
    (a) teacher or other adults
    (b) other children
    (c) classroom resources – picture dictionaries, labels, dictionaries, etc.
4 Children practice handwriting skills – letter formation, neat copywriting.
5 Children engage in different forms of writing:
    (a) descriptive writing – reporting, recording, describing factually
    (b) creative or imaginative writing – stories, poems
6 Children concentrate on spelling – learning for spelling tests, games etc.

84

Organization problems

Learning language is in most respects an individual matter; reading and writing are skills learned mainly through children working on their own. Many infant teachers hear every child read aloud once every other day, and, at two to four minutes per child, this amounts to at least an hour per day in most classes. The success of this depends upon how effectively the teacher has organized all the children who are not reading – can they get on without her constant attention?

Writing activities can lead to a large number of children trying to gain the teacher's attention to have words spelled for them. If this happens the teacher needs to look for ways of delegating this task – by providing more resources where the children can find words for themselves and by encouraging the children to help each other.

Mathematics

Objectives

1   To acquire and use mathematical concepts.
2   To acquire and use computational skills.
3   To experience the satisfaction of solving problems and the joy of discovery.

Learning strategies

1   Teacher gives instruction to (a) class (b) group and (c) individuals.
2   Children work individually:
    (a)   with mathematical apparatus
    (b)   at questions written individually in each child's book
    (c)   at questions on work cards or work sheets made by the teacher
    (d)   at questions on published work cards, work sheets or in textbooks
    (e)   at questions written on blackboard or poster.
3   Groups of children work cooperatively with apparatus or at games.
4   Children work (a) in the classroom, or (b) 'on location' (i.e. counting traffic from the school yard or measuring the hall).

Organizational problems

Children learn mathematics at different rates and need much individual attention. In effect each child is continually going through the sequence of problem-struggle-success. If the problem is too simple the struggle is trivial, there is little sense of success and the child loses interest; if the problem is too hard the struggle seems endless, the child experiences defeat instead of success and again loses interest. The art of the teacher is in giving mathematics activities to children which lead to success. More than for any other subject in the primary school, in mathematics the teacher needs to have a clear scheme of work through which the children move and he needs to be very familiar with the many difficulties that children can meet in working through the scheme.

In organizational terms the teacher needs to so arrange the affairs of his class that he can, from time to time, concentrate on the mathematical difficulties of individual children, either in a group setting or on their own.

Thematic studies

The term 'thematic studies' is used here to include the whole range of activities encountered in primary schools in which topics, projects or subjects with scientific, geographic, historical, environmental, Biblical or general knowledge themes are carried out, with the main aim of focusing on the subject matter and of developing the skills of enquiry. Other objectives are noted below.

Objectives in teaching 'thematic studies'
1 To experience the subject matter.
2 To develop the skills of enquiry.
3 To provide stimuli for language development.
4 To experience satisfaction in 'finding out'.

Learning strategies
1 The subject matter:
   (a) is chosen either by the teacher or by the children
   (b) is tackled by the whole class, or by groups tackling different subjects, or different aspects of the same subject, or by different individuals tackling different subjects
   (c) lasts for a short time – perhaps an hour, or for a long time – perhaps two afternoons a week for a term
2 Teacher gives instruction to (a) class (b) group and (c) individuals.
3 Individuals or groups work from directions given on work cards – either with apparatus or from books; or work on their own initiative.
4 Class watches film, TV, meets visitor, goes on visit. (Visit may require children to respond to work sheets.)
5 Groups or individuals present or display their findings.

Organizational problems
It is difficult to develop the skills of enquiry if people are not interested in the subject matter into which they are enquiring. This leads some teachers to develop only the themes in which the children have shown interest. But this can mean that a great number of different enquiries are in progress and it is then very difficult to provide sufficient resources for the children to

work on. The major organizational problems are finding sufficient and appropriate resources, and programming their use so that the maximum gain is had from them.

Art and craft
Objectives
1 To develop powers of imagination and creative expression through working with a variety of media.
2 To acquire the manual skills needed to facilitate (1).
3 To provide stimuli for language development.
4 To develop aesthetic sensitivity towards art forms.
5 To enjoy both the creation and the appreciation of art forms.

Learning strategies
1 Teacher gives instruction or demonstrates a technique to (a) class (b) group and (c) individuals.
2 Children work individually with media or materials in order:
   (a) to master a technique
   (b) to explore possible ways of using the media or materials
   (c) to represent something
   (d) to make something.
3 Children work cooperatively in a group to create something – large painting, collage, frieze, sculpture etc.
4 Children work at drawing, painting, collage, claywork, model making, boxwork, fabric dyeing, printing, needlework, cooking, woodwork ...
5 Teacher discusses art forms with (a) class (b) group and (c) individuals.

Organizational problems
Many children are more easily motivated in art and craft work than in other parts of the curriculum and are usually better able to get on with work on their own. The teacher needs to find a balance between suggesting ways of working and enabling the children to discover ways for themselves. Organizational problems arise from the availability and distribution of resources, the avoidance of mess and effective tidying up procedures, and the sharing of the teacher's time between the various activities in progress.

Play activities (Infants)
Objectives
1 To experience purposeful, happy play which promotes social, language, physical, emotional and intellectual development. (Children's need.)
2 To keep children busy with worthwhile activities which demand less attention from the teacher than activities such as reading, writing and mathematics. (Teacher's need.)

Learning strategies

1 Teacher either:
   (a) leaves children alone with the resources and intervenes only in the event of misbehaviour, or:
   (b) leaves children alone for part of the time but also intervenes in order to structure the children's activity and to use their experience for language development, etc.

2 Children play with: big bricks, small bricks, large construction materials; dressing up materials; Wendy house or home corner; water trough with floating and sinking things, containers, bubbles, tubing, funnels; sand tray – wet or dry, with containers, spoons, trowels; puppet theatre ...

Organizational problems

Similar comments to those made under Art and Craft apply here. Rules are usually necessary in order to limit the number of children working with any particular set of equipment. Careful tidying is vital.

Physical education

Objectives

1 To develop the physical coordination of the body and body-awareness.
2 To acquire social and physical skills.
3 To experience the pleasure of controlled movement.

Learning strategies

1 Class instructed by teacher in terms of:
   (a) floorwork
   (b) large apparatus work
   (c) games skills
   (d) major team games
   (e) minor team games
   (f) swimming
   (g) music and movement or creative dance.

2 Children work individually under teacher's supervision.
3 Children work in groups – individually or cooperatively, under teacher's supervision.

Organizational problems

In PE the organizational problems are about the movement of children and their supervision in a large space. The safety of the children is a prime consideration. It is essential that the teacher can quickly command the attention of everybody. When large apparatus is in use its positioning is important and there are many points of detail which ensure that injury is avoided.

Section 4 Analysing and evaluating one's own teaching

The traditional role of the tutor in relation to a student on teaching practice has been that of assessor. This entailed spending about one hour a week in the classroom when the student was teaching, sitting discreetly in a corner of the room with notebook on knee, and listing the points of strength and weakness in the student's performance. Afterwards the student received a written critique and a hurried few words before the tutor dashed off to watch another student's lesson. Several such visits during the practice, probably some made by a 'second opinion' tutor, led eventually to a grade being awarded for the practice: B + , C − , or E for fail, etc.

In the concept of teacher-training which is presented in this book, the tutor's role is very much more complicated. His function is to structure the experience of his students in such ways that each gains the most benefit from the teaching situations in which she finds herself. Undoubtedly assessment is one of the things the tutor has to do, but if the grading system is simplified to pass or fail, as I firmly believe should be the case, this activity is only important for those few students who are weak and for whom the tutor may have difficult but professional decisions to make.

One of the most important ways in which the tutor needs to structure the experience of students is in terms of their learning to analyse and evaluate their own teaching. The teacher is himself the prime judge of his teaching performance and his judgments of himself throughout his career are likely to be the main spurs to improvement in his teaching. Evaluating oneself is an important part of teaching and learning how to be effective at this is part of the process of training to become a teacher.

It may be worth focusing on the words 'analyse', 'evaluate' and 'assess'. In the sense in which it is used here, to 'analyse' a teaching event means to identify its component parts; for example to identify the objectives of the teacher, the resources of the classroom and the teacher's strategy. To 'evaluate' the teaching event is to make judgments as to whether the objectives were appropriate, whether the most useful resources were used and whether the strategy was the best that could have been used. 'Assess' is sometimes given the same meaning as 'evaluate' but more commonly it is taken to mean the making of an assessment, that is a professional judgment of pass or fail, or of a grade.

The first of the following activity briefs is concerned with the evaluation of single teaching events and is appropriate for students in the early stages of training. The second brief is concerned with the evaluation of continuous periods of teaching.

46 Evaluating a single teaching event

These are questions to ask oneself after a single teaching event. In the early stages of training the emphasis in self-evaluation tends to be about oneself and one's own performance.

How effective was my educational planning?
Had I identified appropriate objectives?
Had I recognized which resources would be needed?
Had I devised an effective strategy?

How effective was my classroom performance?
Were the resources ready – materials, furniture, display?
Did I project my personality appropriately?
Did I vary my voice effectively?
Did I arouse the children's interest and hold their attention?
Did I know the children's names?
Did I use appropriate language for the children?
Did I supervise the children's work competently?
Did I spot behavioural problems as soon as they occurred and did I prevent them from escalating?
Did I listen carefully to the children?
Did I end the session competently?
How did the children perceive me?

How effective was my evaluation?
Did I identify children who had difficulties or who deserved more advanced work?
Did I note teaching points which could be developed in subsequent sessions?

47 Evaluating continuous teaching

These are questions to ask of oneself during a block practice, from time to time. As with the earlier series of questions these are about oneself and one's performance, but now with much more concern about the influence one has on the children and on the school.

How effective is my educational planning?

Have I developed an effective way of keeping records of curriculum schemes of work, of needs of individual children and of day-by-day forecasts and evaluations?

Have I planned suitable curriculum schemes of work?

Have I been able to make useful and prescriptive decisions on the needs of individual children?

Have I organized the actual teaching programme in such a way that the curriculum schemes meet the needs of individual children?

How effective is my classroom performance?

Have I established good working relationships with the children? How do the children perceive me?

Am I able to maintain appropriate levels of class control? Am I able to establish suitable conditions for learning to occur? Am I effective in securing and retaining the children's attention?

Am I quick to anticipate and avoid disorderly behaviour? Am I able to dominate the class when necessary? If there are any particularly disruptive children can I handle them competently and get them to work at worthwhile tasks?

Am I effective in communicating with the children? Is my voice clear and varied? Is my writing legible? Do I use appropriate language for the children? Do I engage in extended discussions with individuals? Do I listen carefully to the children?

How competent am I at teaching the whole class? Am I able to stimulate and sustain interest in the subject matter of class lessons? Am I able to involve all members of the class in listening and in discussion? Do I use appropriate aids and do I use them effectively? Is my timing right? Do I end class lessons well?

How competent am I at organizing and supervising group work or individual work? Do I give appropriate instructions? Do I keep the children purposively busy? Do I have worthwhile tasks for people who finish their work early? Am I able to avoid having a number of children all wanting my attention at the same time?

Have I used my resources competently? Have I arranged the classroom furniture and the spaces in-between effectively? Have I had resources which need preparing ready before the children arrived? Have I made good use of the display areas?

What are my attributes as a member of the school staff?

Am I professionally reliable? Do I act responsibly in carrying out school duties? Am I punctual?

Have I established good working relationships with the other adults in the school?
What contributions to the work of the school outside my classroom am I making?
Am I committed to the educational development of children?

These are tough questions. If, when you have reflected on your teaching, you find it wanting, draw comfort from the prayer which many teachers before you have found helpful:

Grant me the strength to change the things which I can change, the courage to accept the things which I cannot change and the wisdom to tell one from the other.

Part Two Case studies of organization

Introduction

These five case studies illustrate some of the different ways in which primary school teaching is organized. The focus is on organization: how the children are grouped; what they do; how the teacher initiates and supervises their work; what oral instructions he or she gives.

Although titles have been given to each case study, such as 'Class teaching by "the integrated day" ', it is important for the reader to realize that there are many ways in which these terms are used and one teacher's concept of 'the integrated day' may be very different to the concept of another teacher. A more satisfactory, but more complicated, way of describing patterns of teaching organization is to relate each time interval of the day to the following patterns as described earlier in briefs 17 and 18 (see pages 31–2).

Patterns used by one teacher

1   *Classwork in one subject*: when the attention of the class is on the same work, either individually or collectively.
2   *Groupwork in one subject*: when only one subject is in progress, but different groups are engaged in different aspects of it, either individually or collectively within groups.
3   *Groupwork in several subjects*: when different groups are engaged in different subjects.
4   *Individual work in several subjects*: when children are engaged in individual studies in different subjects and without any regular grouping.

Patterns used by several teachers working as a team

A   *Assemblies*: when all the children of a school or area come together.
B   *Base groupwork or classwork*: when the children whose names are on one attendance register stay together.
C   *Team work – fixed groups*: when the base groups have subdivided and recombined into groupings which have the same fixed membership each time they form.
D   *Team work – variable groups*: when the base groups have subdivided and recombined into groupings which have a variable membership each time they form.

E   *Individual work on assignments*: when children are engaged in individual studies which have been assigned to them, in different subjects, without any regular groupings.

These two systems can be put together. When everybody attends assembly presumably their attention is all focused on the same subject, and hence 'A1' is the appropriate description. All of the patterns used by one teacher working with his own class come under the 'B' description and so can be categorized as 'B1', 'B2', 'B3', or 'B4'. If a 'team work – fixed group' is entirely engaged on one piece of work then 'C1' is the correct description, but if it is sub-divided to do, say, mathematics at several levels, the description should be 'C2'.

This approach has been used in the case studies; the charts describing the organization of a typical day for each system have been labelled with the pattern code.

The case studies have been prepared by me using the rules suggested in brief 19 (see page 33). The use of verbatim passages, captured by a tape recorder, deserves comment. Speech is different from writing. Readers who are unfamiliar with speech written down may be surprised at how chaotic it seems. I have used it in these studies on the grounds that it brings the teaching situation to life and, in particular, shows the kind of language and reiteration used by experienced teachers. What is lacking, inevitably, is the tone and emphasis with which the words were uttered – and thus the affective context is often lost.

The teachers were all experienced people who readily and willingly let me observe them in action. Nobody behaves quite normally when they are being watched and recorded for every minute of the day, but I believe that the following descriptions are very close to the day-to-day practice of these teachers. I have tried to describe the different systems 'warts and all'. The schools and teachers remain anonymous, but in each case both teacher and headteacher have given their approval for publication.

Let me stress that I am not advocating any particular pattern of teaching. These five patterns work effectively when, as here, they are in competent hands. Likewise, other patterns can be successful. But any pattern can be disastrous if the teachers working to it haven't trained themselves to practice it effectively, and in this context it is worth saying that some patterns are more demanding than others. For example, pattern 4 requires a higher level of organization than patterns 2 and 3, and these require more than pattern 1. Likewise patterns D and E require more administrative attention than pattern C. And any team pattern requires a compatible team. Patterns 4 and E require both a broad and detailed grasp of the curriculum whereas patterns 1 and C can be more easily tackled successfully by the teacher who is still in the process of mastering the basic subject areas.

In each of these cases studies the curriculum is overall the same as that found in nearly every English primary school – language development, mathematics, creative work, music, physical education, religious education, etc. These teachers have similar objectives, but the strategies that they are using in trying to achieve these objectives differ widely.

In examining these studies the reader may find it helpful to keep in mind a battery of questions such as:

How is space used?

How is time used?

How are the children grouped?

How much freedom of individual action does each child have?

How does the teacher control the classroom activity?

How do the children know what their teacher expects of them?

How does the teacher know what the children have achieved?

CASE STUDY ONE

Class teaching by 'the traditional day' – horizontally grouped infants

General description

The school is on the outskirts of a small town in the East Midlands. The buildings date from the nineteenth century and are aptly described by the head as 'looking like a cow byre from the outside'. There are four classrooms, each with a high vaulted roof and brightly painted. There is no hall and so assembly is held in one classroom and dinner is provided in another.

It is a separate infant school which feeds three different junior schools, although most children go to one of these. Transfer is in September following the seventh birthday.

A plan of Mrs M's classroom is drawn on p. 00. It contains 560 sq ft or 52 sq metres from wall to wall. The windows are high but are large enough to make the room bright. There are five blocks of tables and a chair for each child. A woven mat to one side of the centre is used for class discussions and the children sit on it quite comfortably for short periods.

In April 1976 there are thirty-four children in Mrs M's class: they are six year-olds. Mrs M is thirty-two. After three years of teaching she had a break to raise a family and returned to teaching a year and a half ago.

Time study: Monday 5th April 1976

8.30   Mrs M arrives and prepares for the morning's work.

9.00   The children come into the classroom and some show Mrs M things that they have brought – books, egg boxes, etc. They sit on the mat at the centre of the room.

9.03   Mrs M   Let's see who's here. Grant?
          Grant   Yes, Mrs M.
          Mrs M   Shaun?
          Shaun   Yes, Mrs M.
          Mrs M   ... My goodness. No one away. What do I put at the bottom of my register?
          Children   Thirty-four.

The register and the collection of dinner money are used for extending number and language experience. Thus:
          Mrs M   (Receiving a purse containing dinner money) Thank you, Elaine. A pound note is this? How much change?
          Elaine   25 pence

Figure 2. Case study 1 : Mrs M's classroom

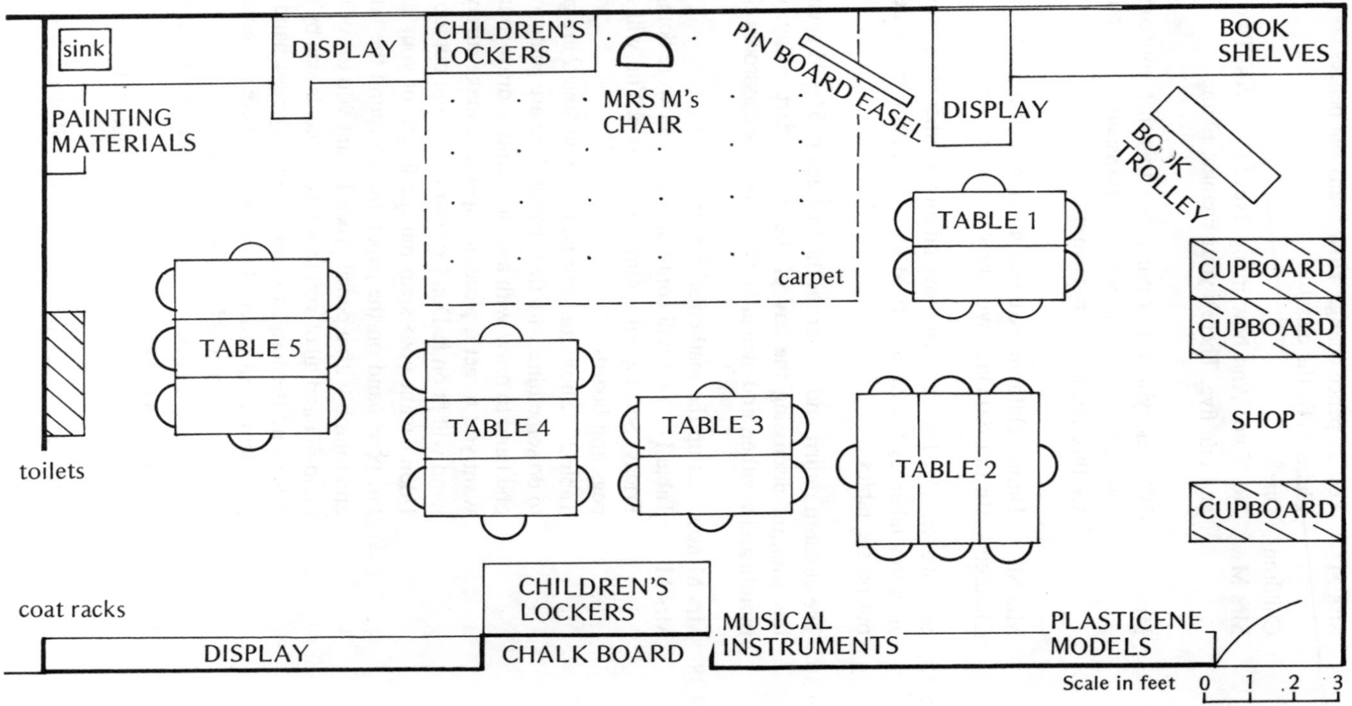
sink
DISPLAY
CHILDREN'S LOCKERS
MRS M's CHAIR
PIN BOARD EASEL
DISPLAY
BOOK SHELVES
BO K TROLLEY
PAINTING MATERIALS
carpet
TABLE 1
TABLE 5
TABLE 4
TABLE 3
TABLE 2
CUPBOARD
CUPBOARD
SHOP
CUPBOARD
toilets
coat racks
CHILDREN'S LOCKERS
DISPLAY
CHALK BOARD
MUSICAL INSTRUMENTS
PLASTICENE MODELS
Scale in feet
0 1 2 3

Mrs M	Yes. 25 pence change. How many ten pences do I give Elaine? (To the class).
Children	One?
Mrs M	No. Two! And how many fives? One. Yes. Two tens and one five. There's your change, Elaine.

...

| Mrs M | What do you call a purse like this that you can see through? It's a long word ... transparent. If you can see through it, it's transparent. |

...

| Mrs M | Dinner children. Are you going to count yourselves. |
| Children | (In unison) One, two, three ... twenty-seven. |

9.15   School assembly. The children move off into another classroom for assembly taken by the head. Mrs M uses the time to put materials out on the tables.

9.30   The children return and gather on the mat again. Mrs M spends a few minutes discussing the day of the week chart – day, date, month, and weather, and then talks about the new classroom clock.

9.38   Mrs M now sets up the mathematics work.

Mrs M	Table 1. You will continue what you were doing on Friday. Sorting out a number into sets. You will need pegs and boards.
	Table 2. Show me your hands. Now table 2 are going to do something with their hands. You are going to use one hand to draw with and one hand to draw round. I want you to get a piece of paper and make sure your hand will fit on it. Don't spread your hand out too far; I don't want your span but the length of your hand. Put your hand on the paper and go round the fingers and thumb with a pencil. Then I want you to cut your hand out and all of you to put your hands side by side. Then find the longest hand and the shortest hand and put them all in order of their sizes. There are seven of you so there should be seven hands.
	Table 3. Sequences. You know what to do. I want you to work with the white cards.
	Table 4. Sorting into tens with unifix on the number track.
	Table 5. Take aways. So you will need counting bricks.

9.43 Mrs M quickly hands out exercise books which have been marked and the children move to their tables and start work.

During the next twenty-seven minutes Mrs M moves from table to table but with most time on tables 1 and 2.

The mathematics scheme is based on Fletcher's approach. Table 1 are using coloured pegs to partition a set of twelve into equal subsets. Table 3 and table 5 are using work cards with problems like this:

Sequences $3 \xrightarrow{+4} 7 \xrightarrow{+4} \quad \xrightarrow{+4} \quad \xrightarrow{+4}$

Counting strips are used by the children to work these out.

Take aways $5 - 2 \longrightarrow \boxed{}$

The children of table 4 are working on the floor setting out unifix blocks in coloured sets of tens to make a hundred and putting small tiles with the cardinal numbers on in sequence.

10.05 Mrs M   I've found someone who hasn't started a card yet. (On table 2: Robert) You have to do your mathematics and writing before dinner time or you will have to do it this afternoon.

10.14 Everybody has now moved to sit on the mat. Table 4 is asked to explain what has been done on the number track and then the 'hands' of Table 2 are examined. This provides a number of points for class discussion.

10.23 Milk time. John makes the holes and Christopher puts the straws in and hands out the bottles; they are responsible for the milk issue all the week.

10.30 The children collect by the door, put on their coats and file out into the playground – except for Robert who is required by Mrs M to continue working because he has done so little.

Playtime
10.45 The children return and sit on the mat. First there is five minutes of flash card practice for the class in unison. The words are from the 'green books' in use in the classroom, e.g. are, engine, sun, into, magic, waiting, stations, sweet, far ... Mrs M uses them for phonic practice as well as whole words.

Mrs M	What about this one. It's a little word but I'm not sure if you know it. (Holds up 'far'.)
Children	Far
Mrs M	Oh good. Now, what is that sound? (She covers the 'f' with her fingers.)
Children	Ah!
Mrs M	If I chop off the 'fe' and put a 'je' what would it be? ...

10.51   Mrs M had collected some pussy willow and horsechestnut buds over the weekend and these are used for class discussion. Words like 'sticky', 'shiny' and 'furry' are used.

11.02   Next comes news time.

Sasha	We played a game of snakes and ladders ... and I won. I got a hundred.
Chris-topher	My grannie went to South Africa and brought me a T shirt. (He pulls up his pullover to reveal a T shirt covered in zebras.)
Joanna	Our telly broke down ...

Each item provides opportunities for discussion.

11.20   Mrs M   My goodness. Look at the time. Right, we'll get started.

Table 1   I want you to do the Yellow Book work cards. Use your writing books.

Table 2   Most of you have got three or four lines to finish to your Peru stories. I can't put them in the story book until you have quite finished.

Table 3   Some work cards to do with sounds. I'll come and see you.

Table 4   Now, you will need scissors and a gluepot. This is to be a sounds book. (She holds up a large green scrap-book with a letter written at the top of each page.) Yesterday I went through some old books and I found lots of pictures. Now you can cut them out, say the word to yourself ... and stick them into the page that has the sound that starts the word. Decide where it goes and put them in tidily and leave room underneath for the name which I'll put in later when you tell me what to write.

Table 5   Some pirates, with pictures and sentences please.

You will need pencils and crayons, all except table 4 – and you will need scissors. (She gives out some exercise books.) Get started straight away.

11.23　Everybody moves to the tables and work starts. Mrs M moves from table to table helping as necessary. During this period she hears two girls read − about 3 minutes each, but interrupted by other children with short requests. Children are encouraged to find their answers rather than ask, thus:

Mrs M　　You want to find the word 'house'. Why don't you go and look for it in the word book in the corner?

Some details of the work at different tables:

Table 1　The work cards are linked to 'Through the Rainbow'. e.g.

```
Find page 9
1   What are the children playing with?
2   What have they made in the sand?
3   Draw a picture of them playing.
```

Table 2　These children are writing their own stories about two children in Peru. Some words which may be useful have been written on a display board and they use their own alphabetical word books where Mrs M writes words on request.

Table 3　These children have work cards such as:

```
Draw:
Two little chicks saying cheep.
Find 5 words with the ch sound.
```

Table 4　They are cutting out pictures and pasting them in the book. Some work on the table and others on the floor.

Table 5　The children here are copying the words and drawing pictures for work cards like:

```
Here is the blue pirate's knife.
```

11.50　Mrs M　　Listen please everybody. It's nearly time to finish. Table 4: Please will you collect the pictures which haven't been used into a pile and put all the rubbish in the bin. Tables 1, 3 and 5: finish off the card you are on now. Table 2: Leave your things in the middle of the table and if you've not had time to finish you can carry on after dinner ... Now. Those of you on cards. Put the card you are working on in the middle of the book and then I can mark them tonight and woe betide anyone who has not worked hard today, they'll get extra work tomorrow.

1.55 Everybody is now sitting on the mat. Mrs M holds up the green book made by Table 4 and asks the class whether each picture in turn is in the right place. They find a picture of a book on the 'd' page!

1.59 The people who are going home for dinner leave and then the others go through to wash their hands for dinner, dismissed in terms of 'people whose name begins with "m"; people whose name begins with "t" ... '

Dinner time

1.15 The children come in and sit on the mat. The register is called as in the morning. Mrs M then asks some number questions based on Easter cards and children answer individually. This is followed by Mrs M showing the class story book – about two children called Rairu and Marilia; the children read the captions which Mrs M has written on each page.

1.27 The major activity for the afternoon is to continue working on the Easter baskets and cards. For this, different groupings of children to those of the morning are made.

Mrs M   Who hasn't yet painted a basket? Just put your hand up. (Six people are chosen.) You six; you will need aprons and will work on that table. Paint the bottom and the inside different colours and don't let any of the box show through.

Which of you haven't yet finished your Easter card? (Three are identified). Who would like to start their Easter card? (Three more are chosen.) Go on that table and I'll come and help you in a minute.

Now, let's have six who have finished their basket and their Easter card. Bridget, John, Sasha, Joanna and Clare you will have to find your baskets and when you have them sit at that table. Joanne, you get some glue out and then I'll show you what to do. It won't take long to get the insides put together.

Right, who hasn't done a basket yet? Gail, Alison, Wendy, Paul and Sally, you can get the handles done. You'll get half of the job done today, won't you.

Robert   I haven't started yet.

Mrs M	Oh no. You get your writing done instead. ... Now, quickly. Everybody go to their tables and start.

1.35   Everybody is busy at the different activities. As the children painting their baskets finish, Mrs M announces that there is space and more children arrive. As the Easter activities are completed people move onto various play activities. At one stage two girls are dressing up, two boys are building a plastic railway, one boy is making a plastic camera, three boys are working with Leggo, one boy is drawing another on the chalkboard with fascinating detail and one girl is playing a tune (?) on the chime bars. Mrs M hears four people read. Otherwise she moves from table to table helping here, answering questions there, and keeping an eye on Robert who is finishing off his morning work.

2.17	Mrs M	Listen. We have 5 more minutes. Please try to finish what you are doing. Be ready to pack away then.

2.22	Mrs M	Tidy up time. (The children quickly clear the tables).

2.27   Everybody moves onto the mat. There are now 12 minutes of talking about what has been done. Mathematical ideas and vocabulary are developed.

Mrs M	Can you tell me how Philip has painted his box?
Lee	He's done three. One in the corner, one in the middle and one in the other corner.
Mrs M	Yes. He's counted in sets of three. How many sets of three has he got?
Children	Two
Mrs M	Two sets of three. And how many holes all together, Gail?
Gail	Six
Mrs M	Yes. Two sets of three are ...
Children	Six
Mrs M	We could say three sets of two. There's a set of two, there's a set of two and there's a set of two. How many sets of two make six?
Gail	Two
Mrs M	Two sets? Three sets of two make six.

2.40   Out to play.

Playtime

2.53   The children come in quickly and sit on the carpet for storytime. Mrs M reads a story called *Witzenspitzel*.

3.09   The dinner money purses are returned and people are sent to collect their coats according to colours that they are wearing – pink, navy-blue, yellow, red, brown, green. Simon is left at the end because he doesn't realize his jumper is navy-blue!

3.14   Mrs M   Hands together and eyes closed.

Everyone   Hands together, softly so,
                     Little eyes shut tight.
                     Father, just before we go,
                     Hear our prayers tonight. Amen.

Mrs M   Good afternoon, children.

Children   Good afternoon, Mrs M.

3.15   The children leave.

4.20   Mrs M leaves having marked the work done by the children today, prepared a display and made a few notes for tomorrow's work.

Notes on organization

Pattern of the day

The chart on p. 107 shows the pattern of work of this day.

In terms of different kinds of activities this analyses into:

Administration, milk, tidying up	30 mins
Class discussions and storytime	109 mins
Mathematics group work	31 mins
Writing group work	35 mins
Creative work and play activities	52 mins
School assembly	15 mins
Play times	28 mins
	5 hours

Mrs M felt that this was a typical day although the amount of time spent in class discussion varies according to what arises. Each of the three sessions of the day always begins with a discussion on the mat, but they do not always end, as this time, on the mat.

The first morning session is for mathematics work which consists of groups working through the Fletcher scheme as on the observed day for three or four sessions of each week. The other sessions involve enrichment activities from Fletcher, e.g. pictograms, work with sets etc.

The second session of the day, after morning playtime, varies. About two days a week follow the pattern of the observed day, while about three days a week entail everybody engaged in a comprehension exercise, copy writing or phonic work, written on the chalkboard. Typically this lasts from about

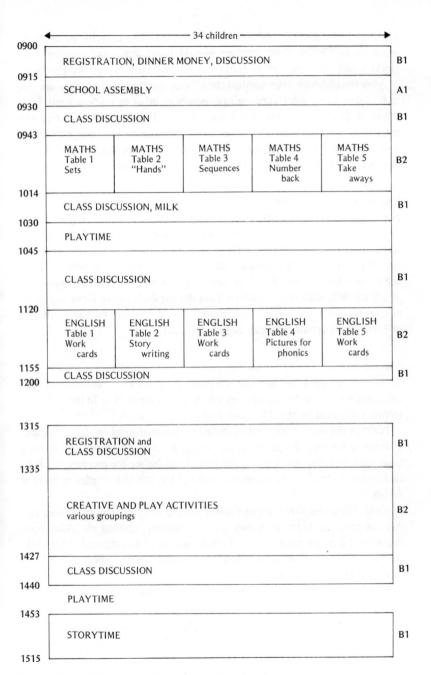

		34 children			
0900					
	REGISTRATION, DINNER MONEY, DISCUSSION				B1
0915	SCHOOL ASSEMBLY				A1
0930	CLASS DISCUSSION				B1
0943	MATHS Table 1 Sets	MATHS Table 2 "Hands"	MATHS Table 3 Sequences	MATHS Table 4 Number back	MATHS Table 5 Take aways	B2
1014	CLASS DISCUSSION, MILK				B1
1030	PLAYTIME				
1045	CLASS DISCUSSION				B1
1120	ENGLISH Table 1 Work cards	ENGLISH Table 2 Story writing	ENGLISH Table 3 Work cards	ENGLISH Table 4 Pictures for phonics	ENGLISH Table 5 Work cards	B2
1155	CLASS DISCUSSION				B1
1200					

1315	REGISTRATION and CLASS DISCUSSION		B1
1335	CREATIVE AND PLAY ACTIVITIES various groupings		B2
1427	CLASS DISCUSSION		B1
1440	PLAYTIME		
1453	STORYTIME		B1
1515			

Figure 3. Case study 1 : class teaching by "the traditional day" :
horizontally grouped infants : Mrs M

107

11.00 to 11.40 and the children who finish the class exercise go on to do work cards. During these sessions Mrs M hears individual children read aloud while devoting a minimum of time to keeping everybody else busy.

After the children have finished the allotted amount of work they are free to do either extra work cards or to choose a number or reading game from the shelf. They can play with this apparatus on their own or in groups and usually do so on the mat. In winter a radio singing programme, movement and dance, and a piano singing session are fitted in the week, whilst during the summer term there is PE once or twice a week outside.

Grouping of the children

For mathematics and writing the children are divided into five groups and sit at the five tables. These groups were established in September on the basis of achievement in mathematics in the reception class in the previous year. By and large they correlate with age and the children on tables 1 and 2 are those who will transfer to the junior school next year, while tables 3, 4 and 5 will join with other children from the parallel class to form 'top class' and spend one more year in this school. Mrs M does not reckon to change children from group to group during the year.

Classroom rules

This term is used to describe the various guidelines, constraints and expectations which the teacher has adopted, and made clear to the children, in order to organize the day-by-day affairs of the class.

Perhaps the most important guideline is that mornings are for work and afternoons for play. A specific amount of work in mathematics and writing is set each morning and if this is not completed during the morning it has to be finished in the afternoon and so some of the creative or play activity is forfeit.

Apart from this there are just a few simple rules related to tidiness etc. Aprons must be worn for messy work – painting, glueing etc. After milk drinking the tables must be wiped clean and the cloth returned to the sink. At the end of the afternoon the shelves, book corner, shop and pile of newspapers must be left tidy.

Mrs M commented on this in our follow up discussion:

Mrs M   The children know that they have got to work in the morning if they want to play in the afternoon. They seem to accept it. I think children do. I think in some places there is too much freedom given them; children like a set of rules. They like to work within a framework. It gives them a feeling of security.

Organization of 3 Rs work

Mathematics

All four classes in the school use the Fletcher approach. Mrs M has a double page chart in her notebook which is a record of the progress made by her five groups through about twenty items of the Fletcher syllabus. The school has a large stock of work cards which are the Fletcher work books copied onto card and each teacher draws from this basic stock as necessary and in addition makes her own supplementary cards as she finds necessary. Mrs M found that the Fletcher scheme needs to be supplemented on the practical side.

The work of her five groups on any one day is carefully arranged so that she can concentrate her attention on tables which are starting new work. On the day of the time study she spent most of her time with tables 1 and 2.

Reading

There are four different reading schemes in use in this class: Pirate, Ladybird, Through the Rainbow and Kathy and Mark. Mrs M has a double page chart in her notebook which is virtually a record and reading scheme for each child; she varies the scheme according to the competence and likely interests of the individual.

Each child is heard to read aloud twice a week. The welfare assistant hears some of the more competent readers on one of these occasions. Also with the better readers Mrs M groups them in pairs or trios and they read aloud in turn in the group. Once children have some fluency she puts an emphasis on understanding and so asks the reader to talk about what he has read. The children take their reading books home at night.

Apart from reading books there are many other occasions in the day for reading – work cards, flash cards, displays, charts etc.

Writing

Each child has a word book for collecting words that he can't spell when he is writing; Mrs M expects this to be opened at the initial sound page when a child brings it to her for a word. There are also picture dictionaries and word lists around the room, according to the topics under discussion.

The stimulus for writing comes from many sources. The Peru stories which feature in the time study started from a Time and Tune radio programme. Assembly themes, events of the year, news of the weekend and things brought into the classroom all provide starting points.

Comprehension work cards are used extensively, and Mrs M keeps a record of which tables have worked through which cards.

Organization of materials

For each session of the morning there are work cards and other materials to arrange. Mrs M checks the paint pots, glue and pencils once a day. Each week she prepares about twenty flash cards linked to the reading schemes. Various jobs are allocated once a week: two people for milk, one to change the calendar, one to remember the dinner numbers each day.

About once a month Mrs M reckons to check the supply of sticky back paper, coloured tissues, drawing paper etc. and to change some of the books in the library. Wall displays stay up for about a month.

On most days Mrs M spends about half an hour before school and an hour afterwards in the classroom preparing work, marking, planning, keeping records and taking down and replacing displays. Rough plans for each day are written on a small note pad.

Children's lockers

Each child has his own drawer in a set of lockers. It contains: writing book, number book, word book, reading book, and from time to time a writing book on a specific topic such as Bible stories, nature, or people at work etc.

Records

Mrs M keeps these records:

> tick list of reading heard day by day; record of books each child has read; group record of stages in the mathematics scheme; group record of language comprehension cards tackled; record of class discussion topics and wall displays through the year.

At the end of the year she will make out a record sheet for each child for the information of the next teacher. This will give an indication of achievement in mathematics and reading and some indication of personal difficulties or emotional problems.

CASE STUDY TWO

Class teaching by 'the integrated day' – transitionally grouped infants

General description

This school is in a well-to-do council estate five miles from the centre of Nottingham and set in spacious grounds. It is a separate infant school with headteacher, seven class teachers and various ancillary staff. Across the playground is a junior school to which the children transfer in the September following their seventh birthday. The school was opened in 1963 and consists of six classrooms surrounding a hall, outside patio and staff room. The seventh class uses an alcove off the hall. The construction is mainly brick and glass, is one storey and all on the same level.

A plan of Mrs W's classroom appears on p. 112. There is a 'messy' corner, a Wendy House corner, a number corner and a quiet area; in between there are sets of tables for writing. At this time there are thirty children on roll, nineteen girls and eleven boys, aged 5–6.

Mrs W is the deputy head. She has been teaching for eight years and is twenty-nine years old.

Time study: Monday 3 February 1975

8.25   Mrs W arrives and checks on the different areas of her room.

8.50   Door opens. Groups of children come in during next five minutes, some with an adult, talk to Mrs W, take coats off, look at plants which have grown from some of the seeds planted last week and then sit on the carpet.

9.07   Mrs W checks the register and collects the dinner money.

9.15   Mrs W moves to a seat on the other side of the carpet, the children turn towards her and they then discuss the results of the seed planting. Gerbil food and budgie food have produced long green shoots like thick grass, but the tomato, apple and orange pips have produced nothing. A potato in the dark of a sealed box is examined; beans in jam jars have made some shoots and two onions have produced long roots and the water smells strongly.

9.26   Mrs W returns to her rocking chair and the children swivel round again. She spends a couple of minutes revising work on the calendar, which is displayed on a stand.

9.29   Mrs W stands and in the next three minutes organizes the children's work for most of the morning.

Figure 4 Case study 2 : Mrs W's classroom

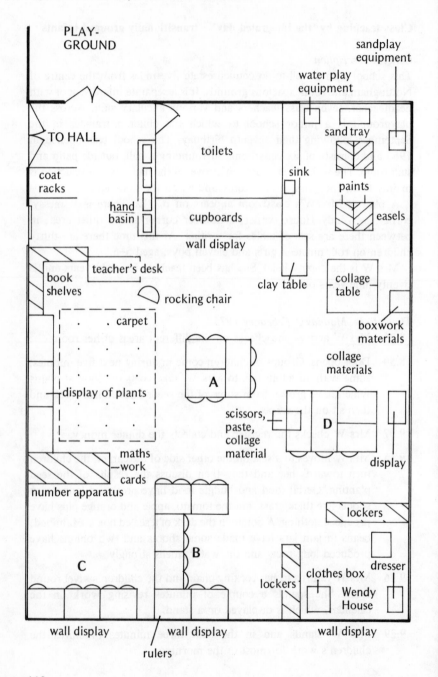

Mrs W	I'd like some help today to make *Our Book of* ... (She holds up a scrapbook with *Our Book of Faces* written on the cover.)
Children	... (various guesses) ...
Mrs W	It is. Good girl. You are clever. *Our Book of Faces.* Who's going to help me make this book of faces? (Many hands wave at her.) Andrew. Would you help me again? And Julie. And Simon. And Russell. We'll have those four people helping me to make my book of faces. What do we want to see in this book?
Children	... faces ...
Mrs W	It can be a boy's face, a girl's face, a baby's face, a lady's face, a daddy's face, an old man's face, a grandma's face, a cat's face, any faces at all. There you are Andrew; there's the book. You four off you go. You start it and I'll come and help you soon. There are some books out on the table for you.

(Andrew, Julie, Simon and Russell move off the carpet to table D.)

Mrs W	Kevin brought us some new clay last week. To work with the clay you must roll your sleeves up as high as they will go and you must have an apron on, which must be fastened. Who would like to work in the clay? (Many hands go up.) Chelsea, Kirsty, Beverley and Tina may work in it first and when they have finished there will be some spaces, won't there? (These four children move to the clay table.) Apron on Chelsea. Sleeves rolled up as far as they will go.
	I want to hear the boys read today. So, Mark and Simon get your books out first and sit in the book corner ...
	Michelle. Remember last week I was talking about the work book I was going to give to some of the very big children? Well, will you come to my desk; I've got one for you this morning. You can start yours off today. Mark and Simon. Just sit down until everybody else is busy.
	Now don't forget, everybody. You've got some writing to do and you've got some number work to do. Best thing is not to leave it all till the afternoon. Plan your day and decide when you are going to do it. Right, everybody busy please.

9.32   The children move quickly. A rush for the Wendy corner – but only the first four stay. Others move elsewhere. For the next forty-five minutes the children are busy individually or in groups:

Wendy corner: Lynn, Lorraine, Jo-Anne, Sharon. Cooperative play partly influenced by a huge pair of giant's feet which have been previously painted and fixed to the wall which make it look as though the giant is above the roof.

Faces cutting out table: Simon, Katy, Andrew, Russell. Mainly individual work sorting through magazines, cutting out faces and pasting these into the book; some interaction between children.

Clay: Beverley, Chelsea, Kirsty, Tina. Individual work on same table. Chelsea made a coiled pot, Kirsty a model of a footballer with rolled pieces laid flat onto card, Beverley made odd shapes with small pieces (I don't know what these were to her), Tina made patterns in a large flat piece.

Writing table A: Christina, Dawn, Bridget, Gina
Writing table B: Peter, Karl, Annette, Deborah, Jane
Writing table C: Julia, Michelle

These children are either writing – about a dinosaur, or about vegetables, etc – at various levels from tracing to word books, or are doing number work cards such as:

You have 6 sweets and you eat 3. How many are left?	Take 3 unifix Take 4 more

Reading corner: Mark, Simon

Bricks: Michael, David, Stephen, Julian

Mrs W spends this period in three activities: sitting in her chair hearing the boys read; sitting in her chair and responding to children who queue up to see her – for help with their writing or to show that their writing or number work is completed (this is then ticked and entered in her 'tick' book); moving round the groups to help here, encourage there, and resolve a quarrel, etc.

10.15   Mrs W   In two minutes it will be biscuit time so finish what you are doing.

10.17   Mrs W   Right Class 3. Put down what you are doing. You can go back and finish your model later on, or your piece of writing or your number work. Is the Wendy House tidy now? ... Hang up your aprons. Wash your hands if they're dirty. Put your chairs under and make your place nice and tidy and then everybody ready for milk and biscuits ... Now, Simon, bring the biscuit box over to here. We won't start serving till everybody is ready ... Right. All the girls with biscuit money come and line up please ...

Mrs W uses the issue of biscuits as an opportunity for number work:

Mrs W	Two halves. What do two halves make?
Children	One
Mrs W	One penny. And she had another one as well so how much did she have?
Children	Two
Mrs W	Two pence. So how many biscuits?
Children	Two
Mrs W	Two. That's right.

Biscuits are eaten and milk drunk − off the mat, so that none is spilt on it − and then:

10.28	Mrs W	Now Class 3. Listen. This is playtime. If you are going out to play put your coats on. You don't have to change your shoes, but you mustn't go on the grass. If you are staying in, what do you do? ... You carry on with your work. And what do you do when the others come in from playtime?
	Children	Pack up.
	Mrs W	You start to pack up straight away because we have only a short time haven't we before service.

10.30 About 8 children have left the classroom for the playground; the rest are busy. Mrs W goes to the staff room.

Playtime

10.50 Mrs W returns to the classroom and organizes the tidying up of the classroom. There is a great bustle in which everybody has a job to do.

Mrs W	Everybody packing up. You've had a long playtime this morning. Everybody packing up. Lorraine go and help with the sand. Put them in the cupboard, Simon. Sssh. Don't want to see anybody standing about. I can see lots of jobs that everybody can help with ... Hurry up girls. What's that string doing there? Throw that

out. ... Lots of paper over here. Come on. Quickly. All this paper off the table. Come on, Michael, you're good at collecting rubbish; aren't you ...

10.58   The clearing up is completed within eight minutes and the children sit on the carpet for a brief discussion with their teacher. They then form two lines by the door, Mrs W having named the first and the last boy and girl for the two lines.

11.02   The two lines file into the hall for service.

11.25   The children return to the classroom and sit down on the carpet. Mrs W sits in her rocking chair. After a quick revision of the months of the year Mrs W draws attention to the clay work, which is new to the classroom.

Mrs W	We have had four people very busy in the clay. Kirsty. Show us what you have made. (Kirsty shows her footballer and announces that it is a lady footballer.) ... Now tell us all about this lady.
Kirsty	She has a necklace on ... and a bracelet and a wig. ... When she was kicking the ball one of her diamonds came off
Mrs W	Oh dear. Oh dear.
Kirsty	− and she couldn't find it and then she started crying.

This develops into a discussion about football and Mrs W recounts her visit to Twickenham of last Saturday. Everybody listens intently. Chelsea's coil pot is examined and then the faces book produced by Andrew, Karl, Russell and Julie.

11.55   The dinner children wash their hands, the others put their coats on, and within a couple of minutes the room is empty.

Dinner time

1.26   The door opens and children come in, take coats off and move onto the carpet. A mother comes and talks to Mrs W about the number work cards that her son is having difficulty with. Informal discussion is followed by the register.

1.34   It is quite foggy outside and Mrs W focuses attention on it.

Mrs W	I went out at dinner time in a car and I noticed that a lot of cars had got to put their lights on. Why's that? Why've they got to put their lights on in the middle of the day?
Children	It's because it's foggy.

Mrs W	It's because it's foggy. Yes it is foggy, isn't it. Look out of there. I can just see the trees the other side of the fence on the playground. Wonder if those will disappear into the fog soon? Have to keep our eye on them. Lorraine. You stand up and go and look out of that door. You can be our fog lady today. Tell me if you can see the trees, the little trees. Can you see them? The other side of the fence – two. Right, come back here now. What number is the big hand on the clock?
Lorraine	Eight
Mrs W	It's on eight. When it gets up to the top, to twelve, I want you to look out of the window again and see if you can still see those two trees, and if you can't see them we'll know the fog has got thicker. (pause) What is fog?

The discussion turns to memories of last week's experiment with a cloud coming from a kettle of boiling water. Later a new experiment is set up with the plants which have grown from the hamster food. One is to be kept in the dark and another deprived of water. Then the afternoon activity period is started.

1.46	Mrs W	Now. Where's my friend Kirsty? How about writing that lovely story about the lady footballer? That funny story that made everyone laugh. Would you like to write it this afternoon for me? I'll give you a piece of paper for it, instead of your book and when it's finished, if it's very nice, we shall put your footballer up on the wall, somehow we shall try and make it stand up and we shall put the story beside it so everybody who comes into our room can read about that funny lady footballer –
	Kirsty	Can I put my name?
	Mrs W	Oh yes, put your name, we want to know whose work it is don't we.
		Do you remember that book that Andrew lent us last week ... Desmond the Dinosaur and at the back of the book it said if anybody wanted to write a story about Desmond and send it off to the people who made the book then we could do so, couldn't we? Do you want to write one, then, Lorraine? ... Oh yes. Not the same story as we read — a different story about Desmond. Do you want to do one about Desmond, Annette?

Chelsea	Mrs W can I make another thing in the clay?
Mrs W	Well I think you ought to do some other sort of work, Chelsea, and let somebody else have a go in the clay because everybody wanted to go in it this morning and you did have a turn and made something that is really nice.
	You children go away and think of your stories. Don't start writing till you've really thought of your story ... Put your hand up if you would like to work in the clay. (About twenty hands go up.) Karl may. Gina may. I shan't choose anyone who stands up. You know you don't behave like that. Jane, I saw some work from you this morning. You may go in the clay. Yes, I said Karl. Make sure your sleeves are rolled up high, Karl, won't you, because it's a bit messy. Ssh. I think we'll just have three in the clay this afternoon. Now the rest of you if you have not done your writing you know that it is the first thing you do because you won't have time if you leave it longer ... If you have not started your writing yet go and get it out and get it started.
Child	Could we make a big book of the stories?
Mrs W	Yes. We could make a big book of them – couldn't we. David, I haven't seen yours. Off you go and get it out. You haven't done your number work? Good girl you go and do it then, and Dawn have you done yours? You have done all of yours, haven't you. Good girl. What are you going to do now then? Yes of course you can. (To story children) Have you thought of one? Well get your word books out ready then.

1.50 Everybody by now is busy. Mrs W sits down at writing table A to give the story writers some words. For the next thirty-five minutes the pattern of work is:

Clay: Karl, Gina, Jane

Writing table A: Stephen, David, Bridget, Annette.

Writing table B: Peter, Christina, Simon, Michael, Kirsty, Chelsea, Michelle, Beverley.

Writing table C: Tina, Katy, Julie, Lynn, Jo-Anne

Writing table D: Sharon, Julia, Lorraine, Andrew

These children are writing about a variety of things and some are doing number work.

Sand tray: Dawn, Deborah (after a few minutes)

Mrs W spends part of the time in her rocking chair giving words and recording when children have completed a piece of work, and part at the various tables helping the children. From about 2.15 on she calls to various children where there is a gap in her tick book – showing that the child has not completed today's work. Several boys move to the bricks, also Kirsty.

Mrs W   (To Simon) You have only written one word this afternoon – I'm not very pleased with you.

2.21   Mrs W   Class 3. You have five minutes left before playtime to finish your work.

2.26   Mrs W   Chelsea, Mark and Tina. It is now playtime. You must finish your work before you go out. If the rest of you want to go out put your coats on.

2.30   Mrs W leaves the classroom for her afternoon break.

Playtime

2.50   Mrs W returns. All the children seem to be back.

Mrs W   Stop what you are doing, please Class 3. Simon, I want your book put on my desk please. Where's Tina? Has she gone out? Well there will be trouble for Tina. Put all your books away. Peter! Don't make a noise. Ssh. Everybody onto the mat, quickly. Ssh ... Tina. I am not pleased with you. You had better bring me your writing and your number work that you should have done. Everybody sitting down, quickly ...

2.54   Tidying up for the end of the day now begins.

Mrs W   Now nobody has painted this afternoon so – is it Julia and Gina who do the paint corner? No, Sharon and Gina, will you put the clay away for me instead. Roll your sleeves up and put an apron on. Roll the clay into balls and put it back in the bucket. Everybody else should know their job ... If you have finished your job quickly what do you do? You don't sit down, Lorraine. You help somebody else, right. Everybody packing up please.

3.00   By this time the children are sitting on the mat again, having cleared up the room. Mrs W, from her rocking chair, invites people to show anything which they have brought from home. Somebody shows a Rupert book, Stephen some keys on a ring, Deborah a finger ring, Michelle has two socks which her father has made into animal faces and which she wears on her hands. Mrs W picks up the idea of this and suggests that anyone who wants to make one like this should bring an old sock; when Mrs R comes she may help them with the sewing. Lorraine has some shapes of paper carefully carried in a brown paper bag. Jo-Anne has her father's car keys; she says he has gone on the bus to save petrol! Annette has a wooden spoon with two faces on it – one happy and one sad. Again Mrs W develops this: 'Tomorrow we will help you dress it.'

3.13 Mrs W tells the story of the Old Man and the Turnip Seed and acts it out with some of the children. Obviously a tremendous favourite.

3.24 Coats on and goodbye. Mrs W stays in school for a further hour, preparing teaching materials and displays.

Notes on organization

Pattern of the day

The chart on p. 121 shows the different activities which occurred throughout this particular day.

Another way of analysing this is in terms of the types of activity:

Informal discussions, administration, packing up etc.	75 mins
Class discussions led by Mrs W and storytime	85 mins
Individual and group activities	80 mins
Playtime or continuation of individual and group activities	40 mins
School service in the hall	25 mins
	5 hrs 5 mins

From day to day, the time spent on teacher-led class discussion varies. On this particular day it was longer than usual, as Mrs W explained in our follow-up discussion.

Mrs W The class discussion time varies a lot. Some days we go straight into individual work; there might be nothing that they wanted to discuss; they might not bring anything in; there might be nothing in the room that immediately attracted their attention like the growing things. They might just come in and sit down and look at me ready for the register.

On this day I drew attention to the clay because it was new in the room, but if I'm not setting up anything special for that day, we just go straight into our work. Especially in the

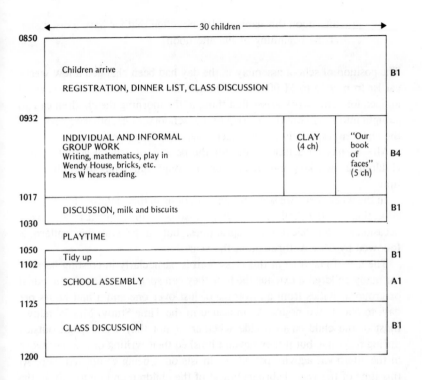

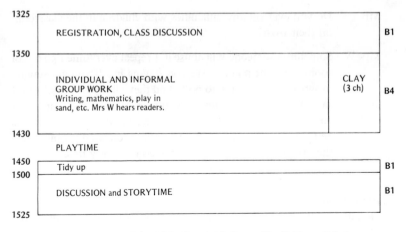

Figure 5. Case study 2 : class teaching by "the integrated day" : transitionally grouped infants

afternoon this happens. It's not often that we have a discussion at the beginning of the afternoon.

The position of school assembly in the day had been changed a few weeks earlier from 9.15 to 11.00. Mrs W prefers the new arrangement because if an idea for some work arises first thing in the morning the children can go straight into it without the interruption of school service; otherwise some of the children, especially the younger ones, may lose interest.

Mrs W has no definite name for the periods of general activity when children are working individually or in groups. She tends to call it 'work time'.

In the week there are some minor variations in this pattern – for physical education in the hall, for singing lessons with a pianist, and very occasionally for television programmes, but in general this pattern is followed by Mrs W throughout the year.

The use of playtime in this classroom is particularly interesting because for many children it extends the time they can spend working at individual or group activities from an average of just over one and a half hours per day, to about two hours. As indicated in the Time Study, Mrs W allows most of the children to decide whether or not they want to go outside during playtime, but if they haven't finished their writing or number work in the afternoon activity period she insists on it being completed then. At this time of the year (February) most of the children choose to stay in the classroom and they work sensibly without supervision. One teacher is on duty during each playtime and keeps a roving eye on the classrooms, but it is unusual for there to be trouble. I asked Mrs W about this.

MB   Do you ever get any difficulties with children in the classroom on their own?

Mrs W   Sometimes someone will abuse it. I repeat everytime I go out of room the same points. 'Are you staying in? If you are staying in what are you going to do?' And they all say: 'Work.' And I say, 'Yes. It's a *work* time. If you want to have a playtime you go outside.' It has to be reinforced all the time ... I think it is better having an option. Some children do need a time when they rush about and shout: some go out every time there is a break, but some just never want to.

Classroom rules
Underpinning the whole organization of the classroom are the rules governing the children's activities. Mrs W doesn't really like the term 'rule'

but some term is needed to describe the various guidelines, constraints and expectations which the teacher makes overt to her children. They are not, of course, written down anywhere, but are part of the understanding between teacher and class. The transcripts in the Time Study show the way in which Mrs W frequently reminds the children of what she expects of them.

This is my list of Mrs W's classroom rules.

(i)   Everybody must do at least one piece of writing per day. According to the age of the child the nature of the writing varies. For the very youngest it may be no more than a scribble picture in his writing book and Mrs W writing a word like 'cat' or 'my house' at his suggestion underneath.

(ii)   Everybody must do some number work each day. For those who can read work cards the expectation is three of these cards per day. For the others it may be individual or group work of a counting kind.

(iii) When the writing or number work is complete for the day, it must be taken to Mrs W. (She responds and puts a mark in her 'tick book'.)

(iv)   Everybody must read aloud to Mrs W at least once every two days.

(v)   Certain of the resources of the room have a limit fixed for the number of children who may work there at one time: Wendy house 4, bricks 4, sand 2, painting easels 4.

(vi)   When any piece of work is complete the materials must be cleared away before any new activity is started.

(vii) Aprons must be worn and sleeves rolled up by children doing painting, water, or clay work.

(viii) Coats must be hung on pegs and not dropped on the floor.

(ix)   Hands must be washed before school dinner.

(x)   Children drinking milk must not be sitting on the carpet.

After we had identified these rules, Mrs W qualified them.

Mrs W   But the rules aren't all that strict. I am thinking of Michelle. Yesterday she decided she would write first of all; she is doing *The Tale of the Turnip*. It has taken her about three weeks. She does a little bit of writing every day on the same story. I think it is quite an achievement for a five year-old to keep the interest going. Yesterday she didn't do any number work at all and when I was checking through my tick book at quarter past two, as I normally do, I said 'Who has not done any number work yet?' Michelle stood up and looked very upset about it, but I wasn't at all cross with her because she hadn't wasted a minute of the day; she'd written all day long. I don't demand number work always ... it depends upon the individual child.

Organization of 3Rs work

These notes are limited to organizational aspects of 3Rs work and do not include details of reading scheme or number curriculum.

Number work

Mrs W explained how number work is organized in terms of three stages of the development of reading/writing skills.

Mrs W	Some of the children are not recording any number yet because they can hardly control a pencil – so it's pointless setting them on recording ... They can't count on their own, so we just talk and count beads and such like. We count milk bottles and the straws put in the bottles. I ask 'How many coats are hanging up?' and other questions like this.
	Those who can copy under my writing, but can't yet copy from a card or book – I write a number problem in their books – I might write just one piece of work, or sometimes as many as five – it depends so much on the individual child. When they have the ability to copy from a card I expect them to do three number cards per day.
MB	I noticed how often counting exercises were coming up in the day.
Mrs W	Yes. All the time. You learn to talk with a number vocabulary. The possibilities are endless. Taking off a child's coat you can bring number in 'How many buttons have you undone now? One sleeve is empty; two sleeves are empty. Is your coat bigger than Mary's?'

Reading

Mrs W hears the boys read aloud individually on one day and the girls on the next. Her system is to call them to her one by one and to work steadily through her list; in consequence there is not the pressure met in other classrooms of children asking if they may read to her.

MB	Roughly how long do the children have each to read to you?
Mrs W	It varies. About two or three minutes. It depends upon the individual child. I've got some children who have no idea about reading yet. They don't know that you start at the front of a

	book and that you read from left to right and that one word is a group of letters ... Other people like Michelle are reading almost fluently.
MB	How does the card system work – the cards they keep in their reading book?
Mrs W	I put on the card the title of the book and the page that they have reached. When they have become fairly competent – not fluent but when they know what it is all about and they are making rapid progress you can't really hear them as often as you would like and as often as they would like, so I allow the mums and dads to mark off three pages on the card – I talk to them first about testing the children on the words – in terms of questions like 'What does that word say? Show me "made". Show me "John".'
MB	What do you put on the card?
Mrs W	I put the page that they have just finished on the card and a tick beside it.
	That's not the only reading that we do – there is more than just reading from their reading books. There are number cards to read, they read their writing back to me, if they can, and we make group books which they read – for example we made a book recording what we had found out about vegetables. I've written it in large writing and they can take it into the book corner and read it.

Writing

Throughout this school four stages in the development of writing are recognized:

(i) The child traces on top of words which the teacher has written in response to the child's description of a picture which he has drawn in his writing book.

(ii) Similar but the child copies the teacher's writing underneath the words.

(iii) The child dictates a few words which the teacher writes in his 'sentence book' and the child then copies these into his writing book.

(iv) The child has an alphabet book which he opens at the appropriate page and brings to the teacher for her to write in the word he needs in constructing his own sentences. (At this time – February – two children in this class of 5–6 year-olds were on alphabet books.)

I asked about the children making *Our Book of Faces*.

Mrs W   These children need a lot of help with hand coordination; they can't use a pencil very well, or scissors, so this was an activity specially for that ... I think some of the children have never handled scissors before they come to school. It also brings in quite a lot of discussion. We've made all sorts of books like 'Things in our kitchen' and 'Things we can eat' which use the same skills.

Organization of materials

Mrs W likes to think of her classroom as a workshop and she stressed the importance of keeping the tools for learning tidy and in good repair. Early every morning she checks her room:

painting area:	Is there sufficient paint? (paint is normally made up once a week). Is it in working order? Is there enough paper?
collage table:	Is there sufficient collage paper? Are the materials ready for use? (Usually replenished once a week; a tray of materials cut into small pieces of different sizes, a tray of lace, a tray of wool, a tray of assortments – packaging paper, straws, tissue, wire ...) Is the glue sufficient and in working order? (Polycell – mixed up in quantity from time to time)
boxwork table:	Check the glue
writing tables:	Are the pencils sharp?
drinking straws for milk:	Are there sufficient for the day?

At the end of each morning and afternoon there is a quick tidying-up session. Each child has a particular job and these are allocated at the beginning of each half term, for example:

2 children wash paint brushes and wipe out the pots
2 children sweep up sand from the floor
4 children tidy the Wendy house
2 children pick up pencils and crayons from the floor etc.

Particular care is taken over the clay since this can go hard and be unusable very easily. After use it is rolled into balls, thumbs pushed in to make a

126

simple 'thumb pot', water put in the depression and the 'pots' are then stood in the clay bucket with a moist cloth over the top.

From time to time other maintenance tasks are necessary; for example:

sand tray:	Dry sand needs to be sifted regularly to remove unwanted objects. If the sand is being used wet it needs to be cleaned off the sand apparatus.
water tray:	(Either sand or water are regularly available in this classroom – but not both because together they produce a mess on the floor which is difficult to clear up.) The water is changed as soon as it looks dirty.
boxwork:	Unsuitable cartons need to be thrown away.
Wendy house:	The tea sets need washing and broken items are thrown away. Dressing up clothes, tablecloths and curtains need washing and ironing.
book corner:	These books are changed once every two weeks from the classroom book store cupboard. (The store cupboard books are changed once every six months. About 70 books are on display in the classroom at any one time and there are perhaps 500 books in the store cupboard.)
bricks:	These need sorting to remove odd items like dirty handkerchiefs.
display shelves:	Dusting.
drapes used for display	These need washing and ironing, which is done by the cleaning staff.

At the end of each half term the walls are completely stripped of displays so that the cleaners can clean them thoroughly. Dressmakers pins and 'Bluetak' are used to hold up displays – not drawing pins.

Children's lockers
Each child has a deep plastic tray with his or her name on the front and kept in one of two locker units. The contents include:
(i)   Current writing book. (Made by Mrs W, or by a mother-helper, with a thin card cover and 10 sheets folded to make 40 pages. Earlier in the year Mrs W makes these of 6 sheets: the point is to

achieve a balance between keeping a record of day to day achievement and the pleasure of starting a new book. The youngest children do a drawing on one page and copy writing on the opposite page; as they become more competent and their writing becomes smaller they put a drawing at the top of the page and write underneath; later they may dispense with drawings and write from page to page.)

(ii) Current number book (similar to the writing book.)

(iii) Word book (either 'sentence' or 'alphabet' see above).

(iv) Reading book.

(v) 'Work book'. These are for the older children where from time to time they respond to enquiry work cards like 'What is a man called who sells fish? and Tell me four things that are red'.

(vi) 'Treasures' i.e. small personal possessions.

Mrs W has a filing box with a compartment for each child and completed writing books and number books are stored here.

Records

Mrs W keeps a 'tick book' as a check that the children are regularly engaging in written work, number work and reading aloud. There is a list of the children down the left hand margin of the page and for each day two vertical columns — in one she puts the page that the child has finished reading, and in the second column an N for the completion of number work and a W for the writing. She doesn't keep this record every day, but about three times a week. She added that if the class were of older infants she would keep the record every day.

No record is kept of individual work at other activities. At the back of the tick book Mrs W keeps a note of the books which children have read, and also a brief record of stories read to them, discussions held and poems and songs learned.

Each half-term Mrs W makes notes on each child's emotional and social development and puts in his record scrapbook a sample of his written work and his number work. She also records in diary form the major events of the half-term: the interests that have arisen, how they developed and what they led to.

CASE STUDY THREE

Class teaching by 'groupwork' – semi-vertically grouped older juniors

General description

The school is in a social priority area on the outskirts of a city in the East Midlands. It is a junior school with ten classes, three of which are located in a nearby annex. Mr A's classroom is in the main building, which was erected about seventy years ago. It is one of several classrooms opening onto a central hall, which is used for assembly and for individual study in a carpeted library area. Physical education lessons and school dinners are taken in a separate building. Mr A's classroom measures 24' by 25', which is 600 sq ft or 56 sq m. A plan of Mr A's classroom is on p. 130.

In January 1977 there are thirty-six children in Mr A's class: they are mixed third and fourth years, that is aged 9–11.

Mr A is forty-four. He originally trained and worked as a librarian. He has now been teaching for fifteen years and is deputy head of the school.

Time study: Tuesday 18 January 1977

8.25   Mr A arrives at school. Coffee in staff room. Prepares classroom.

8.57   Boy comes in to discuss personal difficulty.

9.00   School bell rings. Children come in and sit down; some talk to Mr A. By the time that the register is called nearly everybody, without being told to, has a reading book out.

9.03   Mr A   When you're ready we'll have the register. Numbers please, David.

         David   One sir.

         Mr A   Kevin not here, oh!

         Paul   Three sir.

         Philip   Four sir.

         ...

         (Kevin arrives during the roll call.)

         Mr A   You've made it, Kevin. My word you look desperate. Sit down, tell me about it when you've recovered.

Roll call takes just 60 seconds and is followed by the school dinner list which takes 100 seconds to resolve. Kevin comes to Mr A's desk.

9.06   Mr A   Right, Kevin. What happened then?

         Kevin   I've got an alarm clock and my mum set it for quarter to nine.

Figure 6. Case study 3 : Mr A's classroom

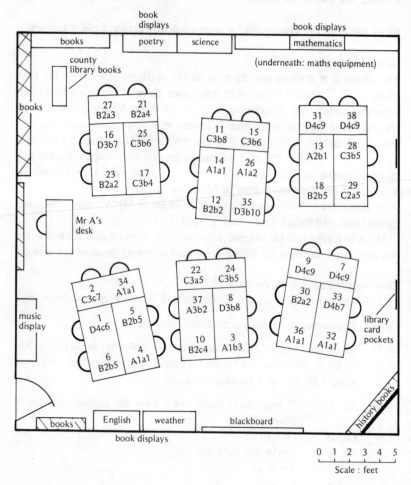

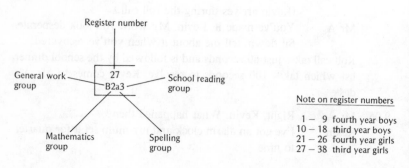

Key to the children's groupings

Register number

General work group ——— | 27 / B2a3 | ——— School reading group

Mathematics group ——— | ——— Spelling group

130

Mr A	Ah! Quarter to nine instead of what?
Kevin	Half-past eight.
Mr A	Is that when you set it for. Oh I should make it quarter-past eight if I were you Kev.

During the next few minutes, while most people are reading, arrangements are made for recording the weather today and for housing a guinea pig.

9.10 School bell rings.

| Mr A | Would you stand quietly please. We have Mr R this morning (for assembly) and after that it's normal reading. |

The children make a line by the door, of their own accord, and, at a signal from Mr A, file out into the hall.

9.12 Classroom empty except for Mr A who prepares teaching materials. He joins the assembly at 9.32 for the notices.

9.36 The children return, collect their reading books and move to the appropriate classroom for their reading groups. Those of Mr A's reading group who come from other classes now arrive. There are twenty in his reading group. They begin reading of their own accord, while Mr A talks to individuals. Stephen says that he isn't enjoying *Shane*.

| Mr A | Oh what a tragedy. I'll tell you what. Give it two more days. You've only read one chapter. It's a bit slow in action at the beginning until the baddie comes into town. Give it another couple of days and then we'll discuss it again, Stephen. It's really not bad. |

9.42 Most people are reading silently but a few are chattering. In a quiet voice:

| Mr A | Can I remind you that this is a reading group. Some of you seem to have forgotten. |

The chattering ceases immediately. During the next twenty minutes Mr A hears six children read and discusses their reading with them individually.

10.04 School bell rings to mark the end of the reading groups. The children belonging to other classes leave and those who have been reading elsewhere return to this class.

10.06 Mr A is now standing by the blackboard and for the next half hour he leads the class in discussion linked to investigations which are in

131

progress in the classroom at present; weather studies, Victorian times and the murderess Mary Ann Cotton, a book on British coins, old photographs of Nottingham and then Mr A draws attention to today's newspaper and the execution in the United States of Gary Gilmore. Discussion of the rights and wrongs of capital punishment follows; only six people put their hands up in support of the execution of murderers as an alternative to long imprisonment.

10.40 School bell rings for playtime. Everybody goes out. Mr A has coffee in the staffroom.

Playtime

10.55 School bell. Children come in and sit down.

Mr A   Will you take out from your desks your Beta Mathematics books ... carry on from where you were.

Books, 1, 2, 3, and 4 of the Beta Mathematics series and of the More Practice series are in use according to the ability of the individual child. Mathematics work is done at four levels on one topic at a time – at present the topic is graphs. Each child belongs to a mathematics group, which defines his level of work, and his assigned work is set out on an 'assignment card' which is pinned to the side of the blackboard. This card gives the mathematics work for the whole class for a period of several days:

MATHS ASSIGNMENTS
Beta Mathematics
  Group 1 Beta 4 pages 8, 9, 10, 11, 12, 24, 25
  Group 2 Beta 3 pages 25, 26, 27, 30, 31, 48, 51
  Group 3 Beta 3 pages 6, 7, 21, 24, 25
          Beta 2 pages 53, 54, 70
  Group 4 Beta 1 pages 46, 47, 72, 73, 74

More Practice
  Group 1 Book 4 pages 15, 18, 19, 30
  Group 2 Book 3 pages 16, 17, 22, 23
  Group 3 Book 2 pages 6, 22, 23, 42, 43
  Group 4 Book 1 pages 18, 19, 46, 47

The children stay in their class places so that each table has a variety of work in progress.

Mr A sits at his desk for about half an hour and about twenty children come to him for help or to have their work marked. For the rest of the period he moves around the room from table to table, giving individual assistance. Only once during this hour does he interrupt the class, to draw their attention to a particularly well drawn block graph:

Mr A   Could you just give me your attention for a second. I hope that when we get some more graphs from the group doing them they come out as nice as this one. It is beautifully done. He's not used too many colours – only two and so it doesn't look like a rainbow, you can concentrate on what it tells you. It's beautifully filled in; he's used a ruler, no lines overdrawn. It's got all the information in.

11.55 At the end of the morning careful instructions are given.

Mr A   (To one child) ... hardly any mistakes at all. Well done. I don't think I should start another one now love, 'cause its five minutes to the end of the lesson. (To everybody, voice just slightly louder, but projected across the room, and spoken slowly.) Will you stop now, the one you are doing, and Andrew, will you check whether anyone is in the hall and we'll have them in the classroom. It's just possible, let's check, that there might be someone in the playground ... Will you now close your book, carefully put it away in your box – in that neat, tidy box you have under your table top ... (the bell rings). Stand up behind your chair now. If you're going for school dinner, line up now. ... Remember what I said about the line, you've forgotten.

The school dinner people file out and then the others leave. Mr A locks the classroom door. He has a quick lunch and then takes part in a staff meeting.

Dinner time

1.15 School bell rings. The children come in, mostly sit down and chat quietly.

1.19 Mr A   Sit down everyone, without exception. And when you're ready, not before, we'll have the register. Just one table not quite ready – almost – yes, I think we can start, well done. David.

David   One sir.
Kevin   Two sir.
Paul   Three sir.
Philip   Four sir.

| 1.20 | Mr A | First of all stand up the boys and girls who are going to go cooking this afternoon. Six of you ... You may go to your cooking then ... Now the rest of you can read your county library books. |

A selection of library books is available. Mr A moves around the room discussing the books with individuals and answering questions.

| | Mr A | Gosh, it's taken you a long time to finish that one, Paul. How long have you had that now? Let's look at the date. ... Which one is that, Shirley. I've forgotten which one you're reading. Oh, *The Case of the Silver Egg*. Tell me about it at the end because it's not one that I know. |

1.44	Mr A	Right. Very quietly will you put the County library books away. Listen carefully to what your group is doing before play. Group 2 I would like you to carry on with the *Do You Know* books. Hands up group 2, there may be a few short this afternoon because of the cooking. Fine. Group 4, would you go on with the dictionary work please – the Red Dictionary ... Group 3, the Victorian topic and poems. Group 1. Somebody from Group 1, Louisa, can you very carefully wheel in the tape recorder cabinet. I'll show you where it is ...
	David	Mr A. Can I go in the 'all.
	Mr A	Yes David. You may work in there.
	Jacqueline	Mr A, please may I finish off my story?
	Mr A	No. I'd rather you did this topic work please Jacqueline.

Everybody is soon busy at their various tasks. Mr A circulates round the room helping and discussing with individuals. He organizes the poems group to make recordings of their chosen poems and Chris learns how to use the machine. This group is standing around the tape recorder and is working together; the other groups are working individually and are sitting at their class places so that each table has a variety of activities in progress.

The Red Dictionary people are using Black's *Writing Dictionary* with its associated quiz book, entitled *Find the Right Word*. Examples of the questions are:

> page 7
> The words you have to find on this page all come from the
> *b* section. The first word is near the beginning.
> (a) Where does a *badger* live?
> (b) Where do you place *bails*.
> (c) *Ballet* is a special kind of ...
> (d) Another word for a *bandit* is a ...

The 'Do You Know' group are using Black's *Children's Encyclopaedia* and the associated quiz books. Examples of the questions are:

> Book 12 (linked to Volume 12 of the encyclopaedia, Toronto
> – Zuyder Zee)
> page 8
> ANIMALS
> 1 What kind of animals are vertebrates?
> 2 Where would you look for a field vole?
> 3 Where do walruses live?
> 4 What sound do walruses make?

The Victorian topic develops from work cards associated with readings and books. Four examples show the way in which Mr A pitches the work cards at different levels.

yellow card

> *Jesse James the Outlaw*
> *Read* the book first.
> *Answer* with sentences.
> 1 Where did Jesse James live? (page 3)
> 2 What was his brother's name? (page 3)
> 3 What happened when he was older? (page 4)
> 4 What did Jesse do? (page 5)
> 5 What happened after the war? (page 6)
> 6 What did they rob next? (page 9)
> 7 What did they rob after the banks? (page 16)
> 8 Who killed Jesse James? (page 22, 23)
> 9 What happened to his wife?

orange card

> *Victorian Clothing*
> Read the back of the card.
> 1 When did Queen Victoria reign?
> 2 Name three ways in which life changed at this time?
> 3 What did men usually have on their heads? What else?
> 4 What is a crinoline?
> 5 Why is the lady in the picture crying?
> 6 What year is it in the picture?

This card has a page of text and a picture cut from a Ladybird book stuck on.

green card

> *Use 'Wash and Brush Up'* (Eleanor Allen, A. & C. Black 1976)
> 1 When Victoria became Queen how many bathrooms were there in Buckingham Palace (page 30)
> 2 In old times, how did they get hot water to the bath? (page 30)
> 3 What is w.c. short for? (page 16)
> 4 What job did 'night soil' men do? (page 15)
> 5 Did Victorians use make up? (page 39)
> 6 How did girls make their hair shine? (page 43)
> 7 Where did they get false teeth after the battle of Waterloo? (page 48)
> 8 What was a mangle used for? (page 59)

red card

> *Use Children's Britannica* (available in the school library)
> *Find VICTORIA CROSS*
> 1 When was the Victoria Cross first awarded?
> 2 What does it look like and what colour is the ribbon?
> 3 Is there any money for those who win it?
> 4 Who was the first winner?
> 5 Roughly how many have been awarded?
> 6 Write the story of one of the winners.

2.24   Anita asks Mr A to mark her quiz work. This is the last piece of marking in this period. He sits next to her.

Mr A	'A beam is a thick heavy bar of wood.' Yes. 'Bisect – cut into two parts.' 'Bulldozer – a powerful machine.' You've got on very well with these. (He reads through a long list of answers and ticks each one) ... 'Brass is a yellow coloured metal.' ... 'Bound is a leap called tied up.' Ah. It's two words 'bound' isn't it. It means to leap which also means to ... ?
Anita	To tie.
Mr A	Yes, 'bound' means 'tied up' or it means 'leap'. Do you know what 'leap' means?
Anita	Like 'jumping' isn't it?
Mr A	Yes, exactly. It does. It means jump. So 'bound' means 'jump' as well. Well that's very good. You really have done some smashing work today, Anita. I'm going to give you another team point. Can we stop for a minute, please. I think after Chris has taken all this trouble to record some work on here I think we might well listen to what he has been catching. Shut the door, Ian. Quiet please then ... and we'll listen.

Everybody listens to the recordings which last about two minutes. The limerick about 'The Young Lady from Ryde' causes some amusement.

Mr A	That it Chris? Well, congratulations on some excellent recordings. You've got yourself a job there; but I expect we'd better have a deputy in case Chris gets tired of it. Very well done. I thought that one by Spike Milligan was well done and well chosen. It needs slowing down I think and also it's worth getting some instruments, with all those bongs and pings in the poem it would go very well.

2.30 The school bell rings.

Mr A	Er. I'm going to collect the dictionary books, so Shaun, can I trust you to collect those up. There are two boys outside, in the library, Shaun ... Once your desk is tidy, and that means there is nothing on it, you may go out.

Everybody leaves for afternoon playtime. Philip offers Mr A one of the cakes he has made. Mr A goes to the staffroom.

Playtime

2.50 The children return shortly after the bell has rung and they all sit

137

down in their places. Mr A looks round to make sure everybody is in and then

Mr A   Ready. I'm going to put group 1 onto science work. Just a reminder that you put the results, or any working, in your science books. The cards are there and reasonably tidy. Andrew will be tidying them towards the end of the afternoon. I'll tell you the other groups in a moment when Paul has finished his conversation with Louisa. Are you quite ready, Paul? Group 3, I want you to try a music card, which we have over here. Not many of you have done them up to now and so I want you to start a new book for them. So would you collect one and collect a card. (He holds up a pile of school-made work books.) Put your name inside. Group 2, I want you to collect the map books, which are on the top shelf and to carry on with them. I think you're on about the third section. And finally that leaves Group 4 – poems.

2.53   Everybody starts work. Some of the science group work in a dark room off the hall with a torch. Others are working with magnets or batteries and bulbs. Louisa is puzzled by finding that when three bulbs are wired in a line only two of them light up. She tries various ways of making the third one light up and eventually succeeds.

The people working on maps are using Phillip's Elementary Atlas and Prater's *Look at your Atlas* which asks questions like:

Use your *Atlas* to find the names of the seas.
Turn to your map of Europe.
(i)   Between Italy and Yugoslavia.
(ii)   To the north of Poland.

The new music work cards have been devised by Mr A. Some are practical and the others based on books. For example:

Choose three chime bars, B, A, G, from the music table. Next, choose a short poem from the poem cards. Try to make a tune, using these three notes, to fit the poem. Write the poem in your music book and write the notes under the words so that you will not forget it. (If you can write music write it on music paper.)

> *Use the book 'The Orchestra'*
> Answer these questions.
> 1 What are the four families of musical instruments? (page 14)
> 2 Name the three members of the string family. (pages 23, 24, 25, 26)
> 3 Name six members of the wood wind family. (pages 29, 35)
> 4 List four members of the brass family. (page 36)
> 5 Draw, or trace, one instrument from each family.

As before Mr A moves round the room talking to individuals and discussing their work.

3.27 Mr A   You have about five minutes before we pack up.

3.33 Mr A   I now want the boys and girls who have been using musical instruments to do two things. First, put down any beater that they are using; second, put the music card back on the music table – they're very untidy at the moment – incidentally, I want that tidying up; and third, take the musical instrument back to the music room and if the music room is in a mess when I look at it after school, we shall be having a little discussion about it tomorrow, so make sure it's nice and tidy. Er, scientists. All the scientific equipment neatly away in its boxes ... all the equipment away please Louisa ... right, come on, quickly, two minutes ...

3.35   I think with the exception of Kerry, who is doing a little job, the rest of us can be seated. Stand up spelling group 2. As you're having a test tomorrow, I thought we might have a little reminder. How about the word 'daughter', Philip? That's alright, you may sit down. Brian, how about 'digging'? That's excellent. 'Dangerous' Andrew?

Andrew   D A N E R G E R O E S.

Mr A   I should have another think about that one Andrew. I don't think you have been learning them over the weekend as I asked. You spell 'dairy' for us, Jackie. Yes. What is a dairy. Jackie? ... Thank you. The rest of you sit down. The test will be tomorrow, so be ready for it.

Without further comment Mr A moves across the classroom, opens Ted Hughes' *The Iron Man* and begins to read.

Slowly he covered the distance, getting smaller and smaller as he went. At last he landed, a ragged black shape, sprawled across the Sun, everybody watched and now they saw the Monster begin to glow, blue at first, then red, then orange, finally its shape was invisible, the same blazing white as the Sun itself, the Monster was white hot on the Sun ...

... the Dragon was weeping. If the Iron Man got onto his furnace again, it would mean that he, the Monster, would have to take another roasting in the Sun and he couldn't stand another. 'Enough, enough,' he roared. 'Oh, no,' replied the Iron Man. 'I feel like going on. We've only had two each.'

3.45   (The school bell rings)
I'll finish that off tomorrow. Very quietly put up your chair. Two things to remember for tomorrow. Please can we have some more comics and sometime tomorrow we will have the spelling test that you have been preparing for, so no doubt you will do a bit of extra practice tonight. Thank you. Good afternoon everybody.
(Children slowly leave.)

4.00   Mr A looks after the school badminton club in the hall.

4.30   Leaves school.

Notes on organization

Patterns of the day
The chart on p. 141 shows the patterns of work of this particular day. Most days are similar, but might include craft or a physical education session, swimming lesson, or a class lesson on a particular subject. Mr A arranges the work of the class on a day-by-day basis according to the needs and mood of the class.

Groupings of the children
The children are seated six to a table according to decisions made by them at the beginning of the year. If individuals wish to change their places this is negotiated with Mr A. They stay in these places for all subjects, unless the particular work necessitates being elsewhere, or unless they have Mr A's permission to work in the hall. They are relatively free to move around the classroom, without asking permission, to consult books, collect paper, sharpen pencils etc.

Apart from this self-chosen grouping, which determines location in the classroom, there are four groupings which reflect the children's level of

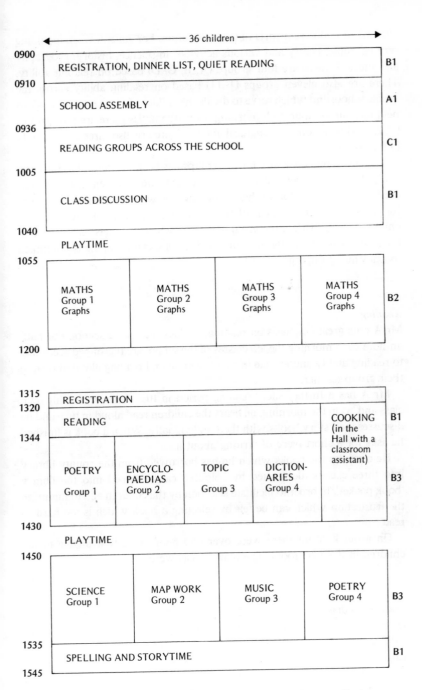

Figure 7. Case study 3 : class teaching by "groupwork" : semi-vertically grouped juniors

141

attainment in different parts of the curriculum. For general work including writing, topic, poetry and various activities in science, history, geography and music – there are four groups (A, B, C, D) based on reading ability. There are also eleven groups (1–11) based on reading ability across the whole school and which serve to divide the children for the reading sessions held for half-an-hour each morning. In mathematics there are four groups (1, 2, 3, 4) based on mathematical ability. There are also three groups (a, b, c) for spelling.

The above nomenclature for the groups has been introduced to the case-study for the reader's clarity; Mr A and the children use, without confusion, numbers for all these groupings, as well as individual numbers for the register. In the plan of the classroom on page 130, against each child's place is marked the groupings to which he belonged at the time of the study. This shows the way in which class social grouping is not linked to academic grouping.

Reading

Mr A puts great emphasis on reading, as does the whole school. For half-an-hour each morning the ten classes of the school are regrouped according to reading ability and engage in silent reading and reading aloud in turn to their group teacher.

Mr A has a further silent reading period in the afternoon for his own class and, as in the morning, he hears the children read aloud in turn and he discusses their story books with them individually. When a book is finished he asks for a short piece of writing about it.

He classifies the books which he has borrowed from the county library into three classes, designated by coloured cards slipped into the library 'book pocket', in order to facilitate selection by the children and to minimize the frustration which can be felt by selecting a book which is too hard to read.

On a quick count there were over 400 books readily available to the children in this classroom. The major areas were:

Encyclopaedias	12	Topics	56
Dictionaries	34	Poetry	30
Atlases	9	Geography	9
English	63	History	18
Handwriting	24	Science	25
Mathematics	45	Stories	89

Other books were stored in the children's work trays, and outside the classroom, in the hall, was the school library with many more volumes. He also makes a considerable use of work cards to direct study in various areas of the curriculum and sees this as an important part of the reading experience of the children.

Topic

Topics normally run for half-a-term in Mr A's classroom and, among other interests, he reckons each year to include at least one local environment topic, something scientific, something geographical and something historical. He decides the areas of study.

During each holiday he spends a day or two in selecting thirty to forty books from the county library project collection, sorts them into three different levels of reading difficulty and writes appropriate workcards.

He puts emphasis on children learning the skills of enquiry and he gives the class lessons in this as well as plenty of practice through work cards linked to the topic.

Other aspects of language

Regular spelling activities, comprehension exercises, 'bread and butter' lessons on punctuation, listening to stories, and poetry – reading it quietly, aloud, and discussing poems, all feature in the work of the week in addition to regular writing coming from the topic and from other activities.

Mathematics

The four groupings usually work on the same aspect of mathematics but at different levels. At the time of the study 7 children were on Beta Mathematics Four, 12 on Beta Three, 9 on Beta Two and 6 on Beta One. At each level the children were working on the sections of these books concerned with graphs, which enables Mr A to include occasional class lessons on the work which everyone can participate in. He directs the children's mathematics by assignment cards, which tell the children which pages of their books to work on. Other mathematics class books are used from time to time as the occasion warrants.

Other subjects

Activities in the fields of science, music, geography etc. develop through work cards. The four groups are engaged in different subjects at the same time. Mr A organizes the rotation of work in such a way that the groups who are least competent in reading skills get more experience at comprehension and reading.

143

CASE STUDY FOUR

Team teaching by 'groupwork' – transitionally grouped infants

General description

The school is situated in a small town on the outskirts of Nottingham; mining was until recently the predominant local employment. The building dates from 1877 and is designed in an arrow head shape; to the visitor it seems a warren of classrooms.

There are six 'classes', three for younger children and three for older children. This study is concerned with Mrs G who works with the younger children. She has her own 'class' of thirty-nine children who are divided, primarily by age, into five colour groups: red – 8 children (the oldest group: 6 year-olds); blue – 8 children; green – 8 children; yellow – 7 children, orange – 8 children (the youngest group, all under 5 and attending mornings only). This 'class' meets together only briefly at the beginning of the morning – for registration and dinner lists, after morning play, at the end of the morning, at the beginning of the afternoon – for registration, and at the end of the afternoon – for half-an-hour of story, singing or discussion. Mrs T and Mrs S have similar groupings in their 'classes'.

A fourth teacher, Mrs C, joins these three for about half of the week to form the team responsible for all of the 117 younger children. There is a rotating curriculum consisting of number, reading, creative writing and creative work. Number is based in Mrs G's classroom (i.e. the room in which her 'class' meets as described above), reading in Mrs T's room, creative writing in Mrs S's room and creative work in a room not used for a 'class'. The children work at three of these curriculum subjects each day. Mrs G, Mrs S and Mrs T each work at one curriculum subject for a week and then move on to another subject; over three weeks they complete a cycle. They meet for a team meeting at least once a week.

On the day featured in this study, during the first period – from 9.15 to 10.20, Mrs G had the green groups for reading, plus her own orange group; Mrs T had the yellow groups for writing, plus her own orange group; Mrs S had the blue groups for number, plus her own orange group; and Mrs C had the red groups for creative work. The orange groups contain the reception children, newly arived, and they stay with their 'class' teacher for a settling-in period of several weeks; they only attend during the mornings.

Time study: Thursday 3 February 1977

8.45   Mrs G arrives at school, checks notices in the staff room, and goes to her classroom.

8.55   School bell rings. Children come in, some with mothers; Mrs G
        talks to individuals, collects return slips about school photographs,
        takes hand of Nicola, who is a new arrival, and who is reluctant to
        let her mother go. There are 39 children. Most of them sit on the
        carpet, chattering quietly to each other; Mrs G tells those who are
        standing to sit on the carpet.

Mrs G   Right. Will you close the door please. Are you boys
         ready? Jonathan. Put your lips together. (The chatter
         stops.) James. Stephen. Joseph. Keith. Victoria ...

Each child in turn answers 'Yes, Mrs G.' The newcomers have to
be encouraged to give this response. The register takes 80 seconds
and then Mrs G goes through the dinner list. That done she initiates
the first work period of the day.

Mrs G   Put your hand up if you are in yellow group. Come on,
         put your hands up yellow group. Right. You are going
         to Mrs C. You know where Mrs C is? Right. Make a
         line by the door, please. Off you go, quietly.
         Right, red group. Where were you last, yesterday?
         Next door reading. So, where are you going today,
         first? That's right, you're going to creative. Make a line
         by the door, red group. Go to the creative area, please.
         Right, green group, get your reading books and go and
         sit on the carpet next door.
         Blue group − you stay here.

She gathers up the newly arrived children − the orange group − and
takes them with her into the next classroom where the green
groups from three classes are gathered together.

9.11   Mrs G   Green group, put your bottoms on the carpet. Right.
                 Who does flash cards in this group? If you do flash
                 cards come and sit down here. (She gathers them onto
                 one part of the carpet.) Some of you this morning are
                 going to work on shapes. We did some the other day if
                 you remember. If you don't listen you won't know
                 what to do, will you. Some of you have got shapes
                 drawn in your book, some of you haven't anything
                 drawn because you are clever and can draw your own
                 shapes.

She gives out a book to each child. Inside many of the books she
has written 'a green triangle' or 'a red rectangle'. She comments to
individuals:

Mrs G   Corrie. When you colour those shapes, do them nicely;

don't scribble. Jamie. You're not on flash cards anymore. Let's see if you can get these colours right today.

9.24   By now all the children working on coloured shapes are busy, others are engaged in cutting their own shapes out of glossy paper and sticking them onto paper, and the orange group are playing with various toys and large jigsaws on the floor. Mrs G works with the flash cards group. As each child completes his flash card practice he joins the other children working on shapes.

9.40   The flash card group is finished. Mrs G spends the next thirty-five minutes in hearing 9 children read aloud and in generally supervising the work in progress. When the children have finished their writing task on shapes to Mrs G's satisfaction they can choose an activity such as straw models, bricks, jigsaws, cars, etc.

10.10   Mrs G tells the children to tidy up and she supervises the putting away of the various pieces of equipment used during the morning. The milk arrives and is drunk by the children once they have done their tidying-up job.

Mrs G   Right. Let me see you sitting up straight with your arms folded. Tuck all these chairs under this table. Suzanne pick up that crayon. Philip put these brushes into the paint pot. Right. Listen to me. It's a wet playtime. So what you'll have to do is go to the toilet, then go straight into the Hall and you'll have to be very quiet. (She makes special arrangements for the orange group.) Off you go.

10.20   Playtime. Coffee in the staff room. Children in the hall.

10.35   The children and Mrs G return to her classroom.

Mrs G   Make a line to go for prayers. Corrie is last today. What do you do if you are last? (Several children answer.) Switch the lights off and close the door. Now when we go to prayers we don't take our toys and we don't take our books. And when we go into prayers we keep our lips together so that we can hear the music.

She checks that the orange children are looked after by children who know the routine and then she leads the crocodile to the hall. She leaves them there and returns to Mrs S's classroom for a discussion with the other three teachers of their plans for the younger children for the next week. This planning meeting is a

146

regular feature of Thursday mornings and takes place while the head has the children for assembly.

11.05   The children of Mrs G's 'class' return to her classroom. She sends the green group to PE in the hall; the yellow group to creative in Mrs C's room; the red group to Mrs T and the blue group follow her into the reading classroom. The blue groups are sitting on the carpet.

11.10   Mrs G   Put your lips together. The little ones can do some sticky cut outs ... make me a pretty coloured picture. The rest of you, this morning you can do your own sentences using the sentence starters. You can find a word around the room, any word, draw the picture and then write the sentence underneath. I'll give out your books and then I'll hear you read. Brian, go and get those sentence starters from the back table please and put them here.

She gives out the writing books and during the next 35 minutes supervises the work in general and hears 11 individuals read aloud. When the children have finished their writing task they can choose other activities. The 'sentence starters' are home-made cards with phrases such as 'Here is a' ... Words are displayed on the walls against pictures; for other words the children ask Mrs G and she writes them either in their 'dictionaries' (if they have reached this stage) or on slips of paper.

11.47   Tidy-up time. Mrs G collects in the children's books. The session ends with the children sitting on the carpet and then they go back to their classrooms. From there they go for school dinner, or home.

12.00   Dinner-time

1.30   The children return from dinner and sit on the floor in Mrs G's classroom. She takes the register and then organizes the afternoon. The yellow group go to writing, the blue group to creative, the green group to number and the red group with Mrs G to reading. (No orange group in the afternoon.)

1.37   Mrs G has moved into the reading classroom and all the red groups are sitting on the carpet. These are the oldest children. Mrs G asks them to continue the writing that they were doing with Mrs T during the morning – writing stories about a phoenix. She supervises this and also during the next hour hears 22 children read aloud. As they finish reading they go off to the creative area to take part in a singing lesson.

147

2.40 Playtime

3.02 The children return to Mrs G's classroom and there is discussion and some singing. The day ends with prayers.

3.30 The children leave.
       Mrs G. leaves with a pile of books for entering tomorrow's work.

Notes on organization

Patterns of the day

The chart on p. 149 shows in diagrammatic form the organizational pattern to which this part of the school works. There are minor variations from day to day, but the chart shows clearly the way in which the four teachers share the responsibility for 117 children. Much of the detailed organization is similar to that described in case studies one and two, but it is worth commenting on the weekly team meeting, which serves to stitch the whole programme together.

Weekly team meeting

This takes place one morning a week while the head takes the children for assembly. The four members of the team meet to discuss a four-item agenda:

1 Report from each curriculum area for the current week.
2 Plan for each curriculum area for the coming week.
3 Any individual children with particular problems.
4 Timetable arrangements.

The head is unable to attend the meeting because she is taking assembly, but she keeps in touch through the record of the meeting – written during the meeting by the four teachers in turn.

Records

At the end of each week each teacher writes notes on each child in relation to the curriculum area which the teacher has been responsible for during the week. This is just a brief note on achievements or difficulties.

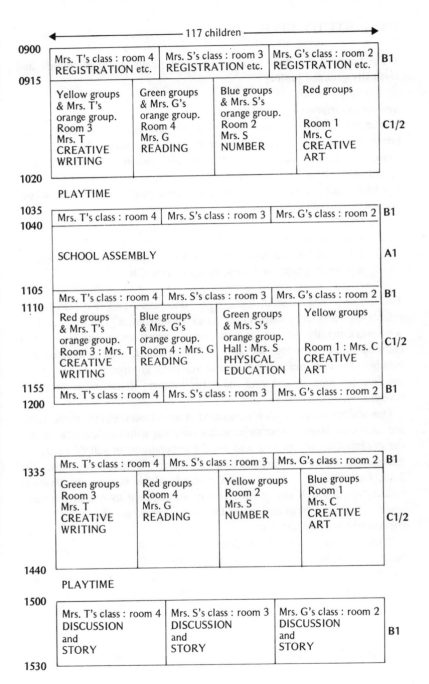

0900	Mrs. T's class : room 4 REGISTRATION etc.	Mrs. S's class : room 3 REGISTRATION etc.	Mrs. G's class : room 2 REGISTRATION etc.	**B1**
0915	Yellow groups & Mrs. T's orange group. Room 3 Mrs. T CREATIVE WRITING	Green groups & Mrs. G's orange group. Room 4 Mrs. G READING	Blue groups & Mrs. S's orange group. Room 2 Mrs. S NUMBER	Red groups Room 1 Mrs. C CREATIVE ART	**C1/2**
1020	PLAYTIME				
1035 **1040**	Mrs. T's class : room 4	Mrs. S's class : room 3	Mrs. G's class : room 2	**B1**
	SCHOOL ASSEMBLY				**A1**
1105 **1110**	Mrs. T's class : room 4	Mrs. S's class : room 3	Mrs. G's class : room 2	**B1**
	Red groups & Mrs. T's orange group. Room 3 : Mrs. T CREATIVE WRITING	Blue groups & Mrs. G's orange group. Room 4 : Mrs. G READING	Green groups & Mrs. S's orange group. Hall : Mrs. S PHYSICAL EDUCATION	Yellow groups Room 1 : Mrs. C CREATIVE ART	**C1/2**
1155 **1200**	Mrs. T's class : room 4	Mrs. S's class : room 3	Mrs. G's class : room 2	**B1**
1335	Mrs. T's class : room 4	Mrs. S's class : room 3	Mrs. G's class : room 2	**B1**
	Green groups Room 3 Mrs. T CREATIVE WRITING	Red groups Room 4 Mrs. G READING	Yellow groups Room 2 Mrs. S NUMBER	Blue groups Room 1 Mrs. C CREATIVE ART	**C1/2**
1440	PLAYTIME				
1500	Mrs. T's class : room 4 DISCUSSION and STORY	Mrs. S's class : room 3 DISCUSSION and STORY	Mrs. G's class : room 2 DISCUSSION and STORY		**B1**
1530					

← 117 children →

Figure 8. Case study 4 : team teaching by "groupwork" – transitionally grouped infants

149

CASE STUDY FIVE

Team teaching by 'individual work' – vertically grouped infants and vertically grouped juniors

General description

This modern primary school, opened in 1971, serves a recently built private estate on the edge of an urban area in Nottinghamshire. The open plan 'hollow square' design accommodates 300 pupils and ten teachers, including the head.

The head, Mr E, laid down two simple and clear guidelines when the school opened:

(i)   Learning, not teaching situations;
(ii) Self-discipline, independence, freedom of speech and movement; self-competition – no cups, prizes or rewards.

The school is organized in three areas: one infant and two junior. The infants are vertically grouped (5–7 years) in four bases. The four teachers who work mainly with the infants operate cooperatively and rotate on a daily basis round the four working spaces – reading, writing, creative and number. The two junior areas are also vertically grouped (7–11 years) and the two teachers in one and the three teachers in the other work as cooperative units.

One teacher in each area is designated as team leader, but the three teams are each collectively responsible, in consultation with the headmaster, for the organization of learning and for the expenditure of school funds for materials. Each teacher also acts as a consultant to colleagues in a specialist field, for example – music, science, road safety, needlecraft, physical education. Although staff have a major commitment to one of the three areas, there are regular opportunities to work in the other areas, particularly in specialist fields.

There are no regular school assemblies, the early morning meetings in bases serving the need for corporate gatherings. There are no designated play times at mid-morning or mid-afternoon, but children are free to take breaks in their work when they choose. During dinner time children are allowed inside the buildings, provided that they are purposively occupied.

A large number of parents participate in the work of the school, helping with reading, pottery, needlecraft, cooking, etc. They are also encouraged to come into school from time to time to examine their children's work and to discuss it with the teachers. Instead of open days there is 'open house'; no appointment is necessary. When a parent arrives, the school secretary finds the child, who then welcomes his parent, gets out his tray of work for inspection and shows his parent round the school if this is a first visit. Later a teacher joins them for a discussion.

The fact that individual work is in progress for most of the time is clearly evident to any visitor. Children are working on their own or in small groups throughout the school and each teacher spends most of his or her time in working with individuals.

The major groupings of children during a typical day

The chart on p. 152 shows that for a short time at the beginning and end of the day, children are grouped into nine base areas, but for most of the day they are working individually or in groups in three distinct areas known as Infant (5–7 years), Junior 1 (7–11 years) and Junior 2 (7–11 years). The groups are formed for instruction in mathematics, for physical education and for some of the creative art work. From time to time, as necessary, area meetings are held, and on infrequent occasions a meeting of the whole school assembles.

Individual learning is the predominant activity of this school. It is organized by an assignment, or job system.

The assignment system

In the infant area, each child is expected to do four jobs per day – one in each of number, writing, reading and creative. These are monitored by the teachers on a daily checklist. The older infants are given a job card each, so that they can begin to learn to keep their own record of work done. Jobs in number are based on problems displayed on wall charts and also on small work cards. Jobs in writing are based on colourful wall displays about selected topics.

Throughout the school, wall charts of problems, wall displays on topics and work cards provide the stimulus for work in mathematics and writing. Children engage in these independently and then take their completed work to a teacher for marking.

The two junior areas have slightly different ways of monitoring the assignments. The following description refers to Area 1. Figure 10 is an attempt to represent the flow of child activity in terms of the stimulus, support, monitoring and storage of work.

Each Friday afternoon there are job checkups – one teacher with the third and fourth years and the other teacher with the first and second years. Each pupil in turn gives the teacher his completed job sheet for the week and this is quickly checked over by the teacher. A good effort is praised, but anyone who has been idle is admonished. A new sheet is then issued for the next week with a requirement of jobs to be done in each area of the

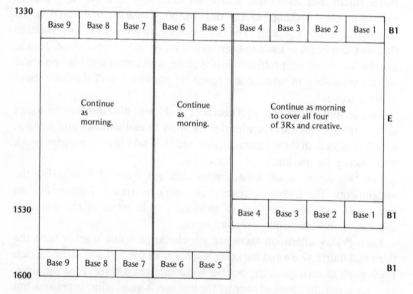

Figure 9. Case study 5 : team teaching by "individual work"
— vertically grouped infants and vertically grouped juniors

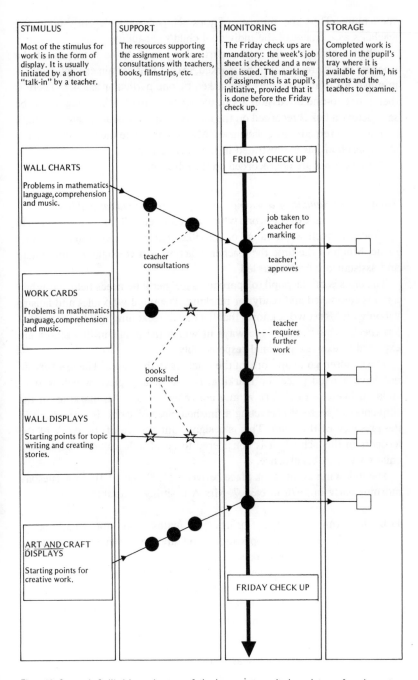

STIMULUS	SUPPORT	MONITORING	STORAGE
Most of the stimulus for work is in the form of display. It is usually initiated by a short "talk-in" by a teacher.	The resources supporting the assignment work are: consultations with teachers, books, filmstrips, etc.	The Friday check ups are mandatory: the week's job sheet is checked and a new one issued. The marking of assignments is at pupil's initiative, provided that it is done before the Friday check up.	Completed work is stored in the pupil's tray where it is available for him, his parents and the teachers to examine.

FRIDAY CHECK UP

WALL CHARTS

Problems in mathematics language, comprehension and music.

teacher consultations

job taken to teacher for marking

teacher approves

WORK CARDS

Problems in mathematics language, comprehension and music.

teacher requires further work

books consulted

WALL DISPLAYS

Starting points for topic writing and creating stories.

ART AND CRAFT DISPLAYS

Starting points for creative work.

FRIDAY CHECK UP

Figure 10. Case study 5 : Week by week pattern of stimulus, support, monitoring and storage for assignments

curriculum. Thus the number of jobs set per week depends upon the teacher's assessment of the individual child's capability.

When a child has finished a particular job he takes it to any of the teachers in his area for it to be marked, except that certain specialist jobs – in music for example – may be marked by one particular teacher. There is then a one-to-one discussion about the work; if the teacher judges it to be satisfactory a tick is recorded on the job sheet; if it is not adequate, the pupil is sent off to remedy the deficiencies. Much of the time the teacher is acting as a consultant, as is illustrated in the next section.

PE and Games are not recorded on the job sheet.

A ten-minute sample of a teacher working with individual children
This is an example of the work which the children call 'marking'; it clearly embraces a much wider range of activities than is usually implied by that name. Much of the time the teacher is acting as a consultant, giving help and assistance when requested.

The onus is on the pupil to approach a teacher if he needs help and when a job is completed and ready for marking. The pupil who idles and fails to get on with his set work knows that the day of reckoning will be the weekly job check! This is one of the ways in which the pupils in this school are expected to exercise personal responsibility.

The children go to any one of the teachers in their area. The teachers do not have a fixed place for marking, but sit at any place which is free; children likewise can work at any convenient place. All marking, in the conventional sense of correcting a finished piece of work, is carried out in the presence of the child. This is a significant feature of the work of the teachers in this school; it is considered to be of little value to examine a child's work in his absence.

The following events took place between 11.00 and 11.10 on a Tuesday morning early in 1976 in base 7. Mrs A is sitting at a table.

11.00.00	Ann	Ann brings a maths job for marking –
	75 secs	multiplications and divisions; but there are some mistakes:
	Mrs A	See here, Ann. Seven into 36 does go five times, but there's one left over, isn't there. So that one must go there by your four, so now it's seven into fourteen, which is two. O.K.? Can you just go and look at those again. It's just that row.
11.01.15	Brian	Brian was heard to say something rude and is sent
	25 secs	off to apologise.

11.01.40	Carol	Carol has brought a story to be marked.
	25 secs	
	Mrs A	... good. Your stories are lovely. Now, what about your topic? Have you finished it yet?
	Carol	I'm on deserts.
	Mrs A	Well finish it off today.
11.02.40	Denise	Denise is in difficulties with rounding off big
	90 secs	numbers.
	Denise	I wondered if that one was right.
	Mrs A	You're rounding off to the nearest thousand. O.K. So if you've got something like six thousand five hundred and ninety six, is it nearer six thousand or seven thousand?
	Denise	Six thousand.
	Mrs A	If you look at that (she points to 6596 and covers the first 6 with a finger) is it nearer to a thousand or to nought? ... (She writes out some further examples for Denise.) Go and round these off to the nearest thousand.
11.03.35	Mr B	Mr B (another teacher) asks a quick question to
	15 secs	check on the organization of a later activity.
11.03.50	Edward	Edward asks where the brass weights are and is
	15 secs	advised to look in the cupboard in the maths area.
11.04.05	Fionna	Fionna asks for the spelling of 'moisture'. Like
	5 secs	Carol she is writing about deserts.
11.04.00	Gary	Gary reports that he has finished colouring a picture
	15 secs	for his topic. Mrs A tells him to carry on writing the topic.
11.04.25	Helen	Helen has brought maths for marking – 'shared
	110 secs	bys'. Some are correct but others not. They go through them together.
	Mrs A	... Go and do that one again, Helen.
11.06.15	Ian	Ian has a quick question and answer to help with a
	10 secs	maths problem.
11.06.25	John	
	10 secs	
	Mrs A	Right, John. Let me have a look. Let me look at your job sheet as well please. (She hints that he

hasn't been working hard over the past few days. He goes off for his job sheet.)

11.06.35	Keith	Keith shows his topic work.
	15 secs	
	Mrs A	That's nice. Now colour it in. And go through it and spell 'many' properly; that's a very easy word – it's got an 'a' not an 'e'.
11.06.50	Luke	Luke asks for the spelling of 'factory'.
	5 secs	
11.06.55	Mark	Mark doesn't understand a maths question. 'Find the sum of' is explained to him.
	25 secs	
11.07.20	John	John returns with his job sheet and his topic work on Africa.
	60 secs	
	Mrs A	… I've found you wasting time. Hanging around doing nothing. It won't do … Why have you got a fullstop here? I'll read it to you as you've got it. … It's quite good, but you're obviously rushing it to try and get it finished. (She marks his job card.) Have you had your music marked? Well will you go to Mr B and get it marked please. Come on. You must catch up.
11.08.20	Nigel	Nigel brings up his topic cover.
	45 secs	
	Mrs A	Oh very nice, Nigel. … Have you traced it or drawn it? Copied it. That's lovely. Good lad.
11.09.05	Owen	Owen has mislaid his job sheet. It should be in his tray, but isn't. He is sent off to find it.
	30 secs	
11.09.35	Patricia	Patricia asks for help with her maths …

Analyses of teacher talk like this one underline the intensity of the activity. To hold purposeful exchanges with sixteen pupils in ten minutes, and to keep this level of activity up for several hours in the day, requires considerable energy in addition to intelligence, patience and commitment.

Description of a weekly job check
Friday afternoon, 13 February 1976: 1.35 pm: base 5
This is a meeting of all the third and fourth year juniors of Area One with

Mr C in base 5. There are thirty children; some sit on the wall bench, some sit on the floor, others stand. Mr C sits on a chair in one corner with a pad on his knee and two file trays beside him. These trays contain a folder for each pupil (boys in one tray, girls in the other) in which are filed the job sheets of previous weeks of the school year.

Mr C   Who has managed to finish all of their jobs this week? (About 15 hands go up.) Thank you. Who has nearly finished? (Another show of hands, probably everybody else.) Right. Rosalind.

Rosalind quickly crosses the room and hands Mr C her job sheet. He comments briefly on it, writes out a new one and hands them both to her. Rosalind then files the old sheet in her folder while Mr C speaks to the next person. Two examples illustrate the procedure.

Mr C   Simon. Your sheet please. (Simon comes over and hands his job sheet to Mr C.) Thank you. (Mr C glances down the sheet.) What about this art and craft? (At this time there was no date against it.)

Simon   I missed it.

Mr C   You missed it? How did you manage to miss art and craft?

Simon   Yes well —

Mr C   Which group are you in?

Simon   I'm in Group 3.

Mr C   Go and see Mrs D and tell her that you missed Group 3 and see what she says.

Simon   goes off and Mr C deals with the next on his list. Simon returns.

Simon   Mrs D said if there is space I can do it today.

Mr C   So if you do art today, your sheet is complete. (He writes 'Group 3 13/2' on the job sheet, makes out a new sheet for the next week, and hands them to Simon). Here you are, Simon. Right. Teresa. (Teresa comes forward and Mr C looks through her sheet. He speaks to everybody in the base.) Now Teresa has done a very good sheet. In fact she has done seven pieces of topic this week, which is rather amazing. They've all been long pieces. (He lowers his voice to speak just to Teresa). Do you think you can get the same done next week? (He enters up the next sheet) How about the music? Are any sheets available next week? (Teresa shakes her head, so he writes 'None available'. He hands the job sheets to her). O.K. Teresa. Very good.

Copies of Simon and Teresa's completed job sheets and of the new ones are shown on p. 158.

Children leave the base area once their job sheet has been processed. It takes about twenty minutes for Mr C to go through the sheets of all thirty.

Simon's job sheet for the previous week

DATE OF SHEET	NAME: Simon	
6.2.76	JOBS	
STORY	2 stories	10.2 11.2
TOPIC	1. Leopard 2. Cheetah 3. Amazon Village (1) 4. " " (2) 5. Java (b) Colombia	10/2 10/2 10/2 10/2 12/2 12/2
MATHS	1. 2. Maths Worksheet 3. 4. Bk 3 p.15 A	11/2
ART/CRAFT	Group 3	13/2
MUSIC		
READING	BOOK	13/2

Simon's job sheet for the coming week

DATE OF SHEET	NAME: Simon	
13.2.76	JOBS	
STORY	2	
TOPIC	1. 2. 3. 4. 5.	
MATHS	1. 2. 3.	
ART/CRAFT	1	
MUSIC	1	
READING	BOOK	

Teresa's job sheet for the previous week

DATE OF SHEET	NAME: Teresa	G
6.2.76	JOBS	
STORY	3 stories Dick Turpin's Ghost The Yellow Chinese Dragon Part 1 Part 2	9.2 10.1210/2
TOPIC	1. Dr Livingstone 2. Java 3. Ceylon 4. The Jungle 5. Gorrillas 6. The planets 7. Colombia	6.2 6.2 6.2 6.2 10.2 11.2 13.2
MATHS	1. bank 2. sheet) 3. sheet) 4. GBB3 P15	10/2 9.2 12.2
ART/CRAFT	1	9.12
MUSIC		
READING	BOOK	
9.276 JH	The Unwilling Smuggler The Railway Children	

Teresa's job sheet for the coming week

DATE OF SHEET	NAME: Teresa	
13.2.76	JOBS	
STORY	3	
TOPIC	1. 2. 3. 4. 5.	
MATHS	1. 2. 3. 4.	
ART/CRAFT	1	
MUSIC	NONE AVAILABLE	
READING	BOOK	

Figure 11. Case study 5 : Examples of job sheets

End piece

As an end piece it is worthwhile to reflect on the concepts of 'formal' and 'informal' in relation to the ideas developed in this book.

There are at least three important senses in which these terms are used, viz:

   (a) 'formal' meaning strict, and 'informal' meaning relaxed relationships between teacher and child;

   (b) 'formal' meaning systematic, and 'informal' meaning incidental programmes for the day-by-day work of the child;

   (c) 'formal' meaning that the teacher, and 'informal' meaning that the child, makes most of the 'when' and 'where' decisions about his work.

These are now considered in turn.

Each teacher needs to build a relationship with her class that suits her personality and theirs, and which establishes a calm atmosphere in the classroom that is conducive to work. This relationship is inevitably influenced by the teacher's perception of children in general and of the class in particular; it is influenced by the children's views about teachers in general and about their teacher in particular; it is also influenced, to some extent, by factors such as the shape of the room, the arrangement of the furniture and even the weather (children are sometimes 'difficult' on a windy day). Within these constraints, I suggest that a relaxed relationship is better than a strict one, not only because it is more enjoyable for teacher and for children, but also because it contributes to the children learning how to establish good personal relationships. In this sense I favour an informal classroom.

In the second meaning of formal and informal, that is the systematic and the incidental approaches to the child's work, I favour the formal or systematic. Here 'systematic' means that the teacher responds to the overall educational needs of the child (as she sees them) and organizes the day-by-day programme so that these needs are systematically tackled through a structured curriculum. On the other hand, the 'incidental' approach means that the teacher responds to the immediate educational needs of the child (as she sees them) and organizes the day-by-day programme so that these needs can be met by activities arising from the child's immediate interests; in other words, the needs are incidentally tackled through an unstructured curriculum.

159

Section One of the book shows how a student-teacher can steadily learn to act systematically in the classroom. My reason for rejecting the incidental approach to teaching is that with twenty-five to forty children in a class it is too complicated a task for a teacher to ensure that each child develops appropriately by doing no more than pursuing his immediate interests. In my view the careful structuring of each child's experience is essential – and that entails systematic planning and evaluation. I am quite firm in the belief that it is the teacher's function to decide what the child should do. (Note the difference between 'what' and 'when/where' as discussed in the next paragraph.) Obviously the more the child's interests are congruent with the teacher's intentions, the better; part of the art of teaching lies in the search for this congruence.

The third meaning of 'formal' is that the teacher makes most of the 'when' and 'where' decisions. Conversely, 'informal' means that the child makes most of these decisions. 'When' and 'where' decisions are those that determine when and where particular tasks shall be done. In this sense, 'informal' infant teachers let most of their children decide when they will do their number work, when they will paint and when they will write, etc.; while 'formal' infant teachers tell the children when they must do these things. Note that this fits within the systematic framework; there is no question as to whether the work shall be done or not – the teacher has already decided that one! In this sense I favour the informal. It is important for the child to learn to make decisions himself as part of his learning to be an autonomous person in a democratic society. It is also important for his creative development that the teacher, having decided that he should do some creative work, then leaves him free to create. The freedom to make decisions is an essential part of being creative.

I hope that the above paragraphs show that the dichotomy between formal and informal teaching is meaningless unless the terms are defined.

Teaching in a contemporary primary school is extraordinarily demanding. It requires detailed curriculum knowledge and a high order of organizational skills. It requires teachers who can plan, act, evaluate and replan effectively for a class of children as individuals. It requires teachers who can justify their actions.

The discussion briefs of Part One, in the setting of four stages of development as a student-teacher, provide the kind of structure through which one can learn to be effective in the classroom. The case-studies of Part Two illustrate the variety of situations in which the teacher may find herself working, and show how experienced teachers have organized themselves.

I believe that in recent years the colleges have paid too little attention to professional training. Unfortunately too many B.Ed courses seem to be dominated by main subject considerations (vital for secondary teaching, usually of little consequence for primary teaching) and by the four Education subjects – Philosophy, Psychology, Sociology and History of Education, which, although interesting in their own right, often seem to develop as academic disciplines somewhat isolated from teaching.

If the colleges focused more attention on professional training and gave more searching tests of teaching competence than is common at present, many primary school teachers could achieve the high standards which are at present reached by some.

Index

analysing one's own teaching   89
assemblies   32
assignments   32

base group work   32

children's educational needs   26
children's expectations of their
   teacher   56
classroom control   55
classroom discussions   79
classroom display   75
classroom plans   13
classroom observation of children   29
classroom observation of teacher   33
classroom organization   31
classwork in one subject   31
courtesies and professionalism in
   school   5
curriculum subjects: objectives,
   strategies and problems   83

daily forecasts   50
daily records   41
discipline   55
discussion   79
display   75
disruptive child – what to try   63
drawing classroom plans   13

educational needs of children   26
evaluation – definition   21
evaluation of a single teaching
   event   90
evaluation of continuous teaching   90
extracts from a notebook: stage two:
   infants   15, 16
extracts from a notebook: stage two:
   juniors   18
extracts from a notebook: stage three:
   juniors   24
extracts from a notebook: stage four:
   infants   38, 42, 50

first day observations   11
forecasts – curriculum   42
forecasts – daily   50
forecasts – definition   20
forecasts – overall for a teaching
   practice   38
formal/informal – three
   meanings   160
'full-time teaching – analysing,
   evaluating, planning' (Stage 6)   4
'full-time teaching – just surviving'
   (Stage 5)   4

'getting cross' – a classroom control
   exercise   69
group planning exercises   22
groupwork – case study of a classroom
   situation   129
groupwork – case study of a team
   teaching situation   144
'groupwork in more than one subject' –
   definition   31
'groupwork in one subject' –
   definition   31
'groupwork in team situation' –
   definition   32

handwriting – practice for students   71

individual children's records   41
'individual work in several subjects' –
   definition   31
'individual work on assignments' –
   definition   32
individual work – case study of a team
   teaching situation   150
informal/formal – three
   meanings   160
instructions to a class   60
integrated day – case study   111

marking and motivating in the
   classroom   82

'matchsticks' – a classroom control
    exercise 68
'more than one group' teaching (Stage
    3) 4, 23
'most of the children most of the time'
    (Stage 4) 4, 35

needs, children's educational 26
noise 59

objectives – definition 21
objectives based on needs 26
observation of children in small
    groups 29
observation of teacher 33
'one group' teaching (Stage 2) 3, 14
organization 58
organization – classroom patterns 30,
    95
organization – team teaching
    patterns 30, 95

'participant observation' (Stage 1) 3,
    10
patterns of classroom organization 30,
    95
personal power of a teacher 57
printing 71
punishment 61

reading stories to children 77
record book – daily 41
records on individual children 39
resources – definition 21
riot – what to try if one breaks out 65

school notebook – preliminary
    guidelines 9
school notebook – stage 1 10
school notebook – stage 2 14
school notebook – stage 3 23
school notebooks – stage 4 35, 52
stages of training 3
strategies – definition 21
stories – telling and reading 77
'story-time' – a classroom control
    exercise 67

teacher, observation of 33
team teaching by groupwork – case
    study 144
team teaching by individual work –
    case study 150
team teaching – patterns of 32
telling stories 77
tick book 41
traditional day – case study 98

work cards 73

Other books of interest

The Teaching of Reading
Donald Moyle
Fourth edition

Designed primarily for teachers and students, this volume is intended to help all those concerned with teaching children to read and are faced with making a choice between the numerous theories and methods of approach to this subject. The author sets out clearly both the principles and the practical application necessary for obtaining the best possible reading growth for children, not only in the initial stages, but throughout their school life. This new edition has been updated in the light of the Bullock Report.

'Mr Moyle's book should continue as the staple British resumé on this subject for some years for it is a concise, readable and balanced view of this vital subject.'

Remedial Education

Reading Development and Extension
Christopher Walker

Practical advice is offered to teachers on ways of stimulating and extending children already able to read. The author assists teachers in establishing a set of reading goals and suggests teaching techniques and an organizational framework which will help achieve them.

Reading: Problems and Practices
Jessie F. Reid and Harry Donaldson
Second edition

Failure to learn to read leads to failure in most other areas of education and for this reason reading difficulties have provided the focus for a considerable amount of research. Most of the material in this second edition is from British and North American sources, written within the last ten years. This volume represents, therefore, in accessible form, the current state of knowledge of reading problems and the practices employed to overcome them.

This volume is used by the Open University as a set book for the Reading Development Course.

Teaching Spelling
Mike Torbe

This book describes clearly, practically and methodically a way in which the teacher can both identify the underlying causes of failure to spell, and set about improving spelling. Advice on making corrections, analysing errors and common mistakes is offered and suggestions are made for games and teaching ideas.

Helping Children with Learning Difficulties
A diagnostic teaching approach
Denis H. Stott

This book is representative of the contemporary turn-around in attitudes towards learning difficulties. Traditional explanations have always been in terms of low intelligence and specific deficits. Professor Stott, on the other hand, substitutes poor use or non-use of capabilities arising from faulty approaches to learning. This is an eminently practical book which educational psychologists, special education advisers and teachers and consultants of primary school children will surely welcome.

166

Festive Occasions in the Primary School
Redvers Brandling

This book is written with the specific intention of serving a practical purpose in the primary school classroom. The 'occasions' which the author deals with include St Valentine's Day, Hallowe'en, Midsummer and important dates from other cultures, as well as the more obvious events such as Christmas and Easter. Each occasion is covered in great detail and includes a selection of poems, and suggestions for a wide range of practical activities from art and craft to music, cooking, drama and visits. Each section is rounded off with detailed suggestions for a relevant class assembly presentation.

Christmas in the Primary School
Redvers Brandling

This book offers teachers a wealth of valuable information for use during the hectic Christmas season. The Author shows how the Christmas spirit links all parts of the primary timetable, including writing and reading, art and craft, drama, history, cooking, music and singing. Activities to supplement the daily routine are described in detail and will provide stimulating entertainment during the build-up to the holiday period.

A Year in the Primary School
Redvers Brandling

In this book, the Author takes a month-by-month look at the school year and focuses attention on a wide range of activities which are particularly suitable for each month. The pattern of work for the year includes stories, anecdotes and poems, environmental studies, art and craft, a suggested class assembly, games to play, recipes, special interest features and horoscopes.

A Place for Talk
Joan Tough

This book considers the role of talk in the education of children with moderate learning difficulties, and considers how children might be helped to learn through the purposeful use of talk. It shows how children can be helped to think and use language through talk with teachers in activities designed to develop skills and knowledge including reading and writing.

Talking and Learning

A Guide to Fostering Communication Skills
Joan Tough

This is the second publication from the Schools Council Communication Skills in Early Childhood Project. It explores ways in which teachers can promote the use of language in contexts which have immediate or potential appeal to children. Topics covered include such questions as the teacher's role in fostering communication skills which arise during the normal activities of nursery and infant schools. Included in the book are pictures for use in the teacher's conversations with children.

Practical classroom organization in the primary school

To my staff and student colleagues
of York House, Trent Polytechnic, 1967 – 1977

Practical classroom organization in the primary school

A handbook for student and probationary teachers

Michael Bassey

Reader in Education, Trent Polytechnic, Nottingham

Ward Lock Educational

9746

ISBN 0 7062 3665 3

First published 1978
Reprinted 1982, 1983

Set in 10 to 12 English Times
by Computacomp (UK) Ltd.,
Fort William, Scotland
and printed in Hong Kong
for Ward Lock Educational
47 Marylebone Lane, London W1M 6AX
A Member of the Ling Kee Group